James DeCamp

Record of the descendants of Ezekiel and Mary Baker DeCamp of

Butler County, Ohio

James DeCamp

Record of the descendants of Ezekiel and Mary Baker DeCamp of Butler County, Ohio

ISBN/EAN: 9783337281465

Printed in Europe, USA, Canada, Australia, Japan

Cover: Foto ©Andreas Hilbeck / pixelio.de

More available books at **www.hansebooks.com**

Record of the Descendants

of

Ezekiel and Mary Baker De Camp,

of

BUTLER COUNTY, OHIO.

Edited by

JAMES M. De CAMP,

Son of James De Camp.

Printed by the Western Methodist Book Concern,

Cincinnati, O.

1896.

INSCRIPTION.

ᴧ

To Aunt Mary De Camp Wilkinson,

the fifteenth child
of the seventeen born to Ezekiel and Mary Baker De Camp,
and who is the last remaining member
of the band of brothers and
sisters known as

"THE De CAMP FAMILY,"

and who is living in quiet widowhood at the age of seventy-eight
on her farm near the old homestead
in Reily Township, Butler County, Ohio,
and who exemplifies
in her rugged character the blended virtues of self-reliance
and simple faith which
characterized her revered parents,

This Book is

Affectionately Inscribed.

PREFACE.

——•——

IF we honor the filial practice of the Romans in placing sculptured images of their fathers in their new habitations, it will not be thought unworthy to set forth in this fashion the images and virtues of our ancestors.

We wish, modestly, to make a permanent record of our grandparents, Ezekiel and Mary Baker De Camp, and of their seventeen children—twelve sons and five daughters—sixteen of whom lived to become heads of families, all actively identified with the Church, and noted for the reliableness of their word and work, for self-reliance, industry, frugality, and an energetic force of character beyond the ordinary.

These characteristics made them successful farmers, builders, and business men, who spent their whole lives in Butler and Hamilton Counties, Ohio. Nine of the brothers resided in Cincinnati, where for sixty years—from 1831 to 1891—diminishing by death through the decades—they impressed themselves on the religious and business community as enterprising Christian citizens.

The De Camps were loyal to their families and to each other, aided one another in business, and shared their joys and sorrows in sympathizing fellowship. May their example be a constant inspiration to right living in their descend-

ants—over seven hundred of whom have been born since
the union in 1799 of Grandfather and Grandmother DeCamp!

We also give a complete record of the descendants.
We are indebted to our brother David for much of the gen-
ealogy prepared by him some years ago. It is a work of
love, but of labor also; and some errors in dates are quite
possible.

J. M. D.

CINCINNATI, June 1, 1896.

TABLE OF CONTENTS.

DECAMP ANCESTRY.

OUR immediate ancestors neglected to hand down any records, and we have verified nothing beyond our great grandfather Moses De Camp, of Westfield, N. J., who was born September 28, 1735. It is a family legend that three French Huguenots, De Camp brothers, came to America in 16—, one settling in Massachusetts and calling himself Van Camp, another settling in Connecticut and calling himself Camp, and the other settling in New York, and afterward in New Jersey, and retaining the name De Camp. We know that two of Moses' brothers were Lambert and David, and that the father of Moses De Camp was Lambert De Camp. Such a grave was so marked twenty years ago in the old cemetery adjoining the white Presbyterian Church in Westfield, N. J., but it is not now to be found, and the old Church records were destroyed by fire. We find in the registry of wills in the office of the Secretary of State, at Trenton, N. J., the will of Lambert De Camp, of Elizabeth, Essex County, N. J., October 4, 1784, bequeathing pounds and lands to his wife, Mary, and children, Henry, Lambert, James, David, *Moses*, Joseph, Elizabeth, and Leah. Having also heard that Ezekiel De Camp named his sons after his father's brothers, and as six of these names reappear in Ezekiel's sons, we believe this to be our ancestral line. The will speaks of his father Hendrick De Camp and of a brother Henry. We found also the will of Hendrick De Camp, of Woodbridge, Middlesex County, N. J., made June 4, 1771, "being very aged," bequeathing plantations to his wife, Mary, and children, Aliche Lovee, *Lambert*, John,

9

Christina Woodruff, Henry, and Benjamin. A will is recorded
of Henry De Camp, so that the pedigree would read:

HENDRICK DE CAMP,

Born about 1680.

CHILDREN OF HENDRICK AND MARY DE CAMP.	GRANDCHILDREN.
1. ALICHE LOVEE.	
2. LAMBERT DE CAMP, born 1711, Elizabeth, Essex County. Will October 4, 1784.	Henry, Lambert, James, David, Moses, Joseph, Elizabeth, and Leah DeCamp.
3. JOHN DE CAMP.	
4. CHRISTINA WOODRUFF.	
5. HENRY DE CAMP, Woodbridge, Middlesex County. Will October 31, 1776.	Enoch, Job, Zachariah, Phebe Ackorn, Elizabeth Scudder, Mary Hetfield, and Sarah Gilman.
6. BENJAMIN DE CAMP.	John, Lawrence, and two daughters.

Since writing the above, we have received a letter from Mr.
Geo. A. Morrison, Jr., of New York City (a descendant of one
of the De Camp branches), who is assiduously tracing the
De Camp Huguenot line through Holland and France. It states
that we are correct as to Lambert and Hendrick (Dutch for
Henry) being the progenitors of our Moses De Camp; that
Hendrick De Camp was born 1680, at New Utrecht, Long
Island, and was the son of Lawrence (sometimes recorded Lau-
rens and Laurent) and Elsie (de Mandeville) De Camp, and that
Lawrence was the son of John De Camp, who never came to
America; that Lawrence De Camp was the first of his name
in America, and the only one in 1664 in all probability. He
had children; John, Christina, Mary, Henry or Hendrick,
Gideon, and Elsie. He also states that all the children of
Hendrick De Camp are not mentioned in his will of June, 1771.

MOSES DE CAMP

Was born in Westfield (then Essex County), N. J., September 28, 1735, married Sarah Ross and removed to Butler County, Ohio, in September, 1812, with their son Ezekiel, his wife Mary Baker De Camp, and their children. Moses' son David (and wife, Sarah Wood) also came. Moses purchased, and divided between his sons David and Ezekiel, 160 acres in Reily Township, Section 14, Range 1 east, about four miles south of Oxford, Ohio, and lived in the log-house he helped to erect until October 5, 1827, when he died at the age of ninety-two years. His wife survived him eight years, and died May 15, 1835, in her eighty-ninth year, and their graves are in the cemetery of the old Bethel Presbyterian Church, seven miles west of Hamilton, Ohio.

It has been a matter of knowledge in the family that Moses De Camp served throughout the Seven Years' Revolutionary War, being then forty-one years old. His flint-lock musket, which he carried throughout the war, is in the keeping of Mrs. Rebecca Hand Mustin, a great-granddaughter, at Wood's Station. It is family history that when Washington's Army was disheartened with cold and hunger, he made a speech to his men and asked those who would stand by him " to come forward and take his hand," and Moses De Camp was one of the first to respond. On another occasion, when the Tories had corralled some cattle in a field, an officer called for a volunteer to let down the bars that they might escape, and Moses went forward and let them down while the enemies' bullets were falling thick around him.

We do not find in the records of the Pension office at Washington, nor in the roster of New Jersey troops in the Revolutionary War, our Moses De Camp. This, however, would not prove he was not in the war, as new names are constantly coming to light, besides it is common history in the family that he refused to receive a pension. There are several De Camps given in the records: Abraham, Enoch, John, Joab, James, and

Ezekiel. There is a Moses De Camp in Col. Sheldon's Second Regiment, but he was fifteen years younger than our Moses.

MOSES AND SARAH DE CAMP'S CHILDREN WERE:

1. Walter De Camp, who died at Westfield, May 24, 1802, aged 37 years.

2. Hannah De Camp, who married Ellis Hand, and had no children.

3. David De Camp, who died in Butler County, Ohio, August 22, 1860, aged 88 years. He married Sarah Wood, and had no children.

4. Nancy De Camp, who married Squire Pierson, and had nine children.

5. Ezekiel De Camp, who married Mary Baker, and had seventeen children.

6. Sarah De Camp, who married Aaron Sayres, and had three children.

7. Betsy De Camp, who married Jacob Denman, and had six children.

8. Rebekah De Camp, who died at Westfield, March 23, 1789, aged 4 years.

EZEKIEL DE CAMP.

MARY BAKER DE CAMP.

EZEKIEL DE CAMP.

Born in Westfield, N. J., October 4, 1779.
Died in Butler County, Ohio, October 25, 1860.

In 1811 a solitary horseman, at the age of thirty-two, crossed the mountains and forded the streams between New Jersey and Ohio, and selected the locality of his future home on the rolling plateau and timberland near Indian Creek, Reily Township, Butler County. It was our grandfather, Ezekiel De Camp. Meeting Nicholas Longworth, the subsequent millionaire land and lease owner of Cincinnati, the effort was made to persuade him to settle in Cincinnati, and buy twenty-eight acres where the Sixth Street market-house stands; but fearing fevers and having regard for his children, a selection on high land some thirty miles northwest was made. He returned to New Jersey from his prospecting tour, and on March 20, 1812 (see deed on file in Newark, N. J., court-house), his father, Moses De Camp, sold to William Baker eighty-seven acres in Westfield Township for $3,201.69, and in the month of September, 1812, nine years after Ohio was made a sovereign State, when the country was in the midst of war with England, and General William Henry Harrison was fighting Indians (allies of Canada) in Ohio and Indiana, the family moved to Butler County, Ohio.

THE JOURNEY.

The party consisted of Moses De Camp, aged 77 years; Sarah his wife, aged 65; Ezekiel his son, aged 33; Mary his wife, aged 32; and ten children, the youngest, Henry, being a babe of six weeks.

The journey consumed six weeks (the roads were poor and there were no bridges), and was made by horse and ox teams in two covered wagons, the family cows trailing behind.

A big iron griddle, that hung on a crane underneath the wagon, was an object of special fondness to the little toddlers, Harvey and Joseph, who took turns riding upon it. The children took whooping-cough *en route*, one of the horses died, and

Henry, the baby, came near smothering to death in the feather-
bed which hung overhead.   The beds were used on the floor of
some house or under the trees at night, and one morning he was
accidentally rolled and corded up, when his mother in her search
heard his cry and cut the ropes and rescued her child, who was
as black as an African.   Notwithstanding this ludicrous chapter
of accidents, the journey was safely ended, a clearing made in
the woods, a large log-house erected; fields for corn prepared, and
the pioneer life in earnest began.   A few years ago, at Aunt
Hannah's, we saw the well-made, high-back, splint-bottomed
chair in which Moses' wife sat on that journey.   Ezekiel's wife,
Polly (Mary) Baker, to whom he was married February 22,
1799, was a superior and helpful mate, sharing with great
patience and cheerfulness the hard lot of a frontier life.   Seven
more children were born to this sturdy pair in the new home,
and rocked in cradles made from hollow elm logs, until in 1822,
in a period of twenty-three years, seventeen children blessed
their union.   Of such people are the foundations of States laid.

In retrospection, this is a marvelous record.   Such families
are now rarely seen, although this is a rapid age.

We can not give incidents of their long life, their sayings and
doings, their comings and goings.   Aunt Mary says her father
was "a neat farmer."   It is enough to know that they reared
their children in Christian faith and practice.   Theirs was a
house of grace and prayer.   They bore a good name in the
country round about for honor, worth, and hospitality.

They early taught their children the value of work, of industry, fidelity, and temperance.   They got such district-school
education as a few months each winter could furnish, in
music, reading, writing, spelling, and arithmetic.   When seventeen or eighteen years old, the boys went on foot to Cincinnati,
and were apprenticed to trades, as brick or stone masons, carpenters and plasterers, the older ones thus out of the way as the
younger ones came on.   As the sons in the city grew to men's
estate, married and established homes, the parents made them
frequent visits and rejoiced in their prosperity.   In turn, the
boys wanted no better respite from toil than to go up to
the old home, shoot squirrels, drive "old Charley," help with

the haying or other farm-work, tell stories (in which art they excelled) round the ample hearthstone, in the corner of which grandmother sat, with bowed frame, her lustrous, deep-set eyes flashing with kindly sagacity, while grandfather, with his stand-up collar and black stock, his ivory-headed cane in hand, sat in his arm-chair, bluff, jolly, and hearty—a man of noble countenance, of compact and portly frame, and of medium height.

To have raised and seen successfully married and established in Church and business relations, sixteen of their children (young Moses dying at ten) is an achievement and record of which a parent's heart would naturally swell with grateful pride. It was their good fortune, June 1, 1851, to enjoy a family reunion at the homestead, at which 153 of their descendants were present. An account of this reunion, and one of June 1, 1870, after their death, appears at the close of this book.

Grandfather De Camp united with Ebenezer Methodist Church about 1840. He fell asleep without a struggle or a groan, October 25, 1860, aged eighty-one years. His last words were words of triumph: "Come, Lord Jesus, come quickly!" Rev. Michael Marlay preached his funeral sermon from 1 Thess. iv, 13, 14.

On his gravestone in the Oxford Cemetery is inscribed:

> A kind father,
> A faithful husband,
> And a true friend.
> " O, Lord of hosts, blessed is the man
> that trusteth in thee."

Ezekiel's brother, David De Camp, and Sarah Wood De Camp, his wife, lived on an adjoining farm, and, having no children, raised Hiram and James of Ezekiel's family, and ever afterwards they and their families held old Uncle David and Aunt Sally in special remembrance. We remember eating Aunt Sally's good pies for breakfast (baked in the oven in the yard) and drinking dainty bowls of milk. Old Uncle David's blessing was, "Whether,

therefore, ye eat or drink, or whatsoever ye do, do all to the glory
of God." He died August 22, 1860, aged eighty-eight years and
twenty-nine days. On his headstone at Oxford is inscribed the
sentiment:

> "An honest man is the noblest work of God."

A Masonic compass is engraved at the top.

His gold Masonic emblem is in the keeping of Lambert's son,
Hiram De Camp. We have often heard him speak of seeing
George Washington riding in his coach. His wife died September 6, 1864, aged eighty-seven years.

MARY BAKER DE CAMP.

Born near Westfield, N. J., June 25, 1780.
Died in Butler County, Ohio, December 1, 1859.

Her paternal ancestor was Captain John Baker, who came from England about 1660. He resided in New Amsterdam (which soon after his arrival became New York) for a number of years, filling many official positions. In numerous land negotiations he acted as the English and Dutch interpreter, and one of the natives acted as Indian and Dutch interpreter. The conferences were said to have resulted satisfactorily to all interests. After the conquest of the city, Governor Nicolls appointed him chief military officer at Albany, September 25, 1665. In the year 1667 he, with eight others, bought a land-grant of 1,200 acres in Elizabethtown, N. J. He was appointed coroner March 28, 1683, and Judge of small causes.

He was a leading man in the community, and foremost in resisting the proprietary assumptions. He died in 1702. He was the ancestor of Henry Baker, of Westfield, N. J., who married Phebe Hedges, of Long Island. They were the parents of Daniel Baker.

Daniel Baker was born in Westfield, N. J., June 3, 1753; married Margaret Osborn, and died July 10, 1814. They were the parents of our grandmother, Mary Baker De Camp.

Daniel Baker fought with credit during the entire War of the Revolution in the capacity of private, corporal, and ensign. He served as private in Captain John Scudder's company, First Regiment, Essex County, New Jersey militia; was promoted ensign of the same company. He also served as ensign in Captain John Scudder's company of the New Jersey State troops. He was enrolled as a corporal in Captain Andrew McMyer's company of the First Battalion, first establishment New Jersey Continental Line, November 13, 1775, and as such took part in the operations before Quebec (see records of office of adjutant-general State of New Jersey and "History of Union and Middlesex Counties," and Littell's "First Settlers of Passaic Valley").

In June, 1780, when the Tories invaded New Jersey, burning Springfield on the 23d, Margaret Baker was one of the Westfield women who, hearing of the approach of the Tories, fled to Mr. Baltus Roll's farm, on Springfield Mountain, about three miles from Westfield, *where, from fatigue and fright, she gave premature birth, June 25, 1780, to her first child, Mary Baker,* the eldest of fourteen, and the subsequent wife of our grandfather, Ezekiel De Camp.

Mary Baker De Camp was a woman of a high type of moral principle, and devoted her life to the raising of her large family, ten of whom were born in New Jersey and seven in Ohio. She instilled into them the principles of sobriety, industry, and of Christian faith, having been raised in the Presbyterian communion. Twelve of her children became identified with the Methodist Episcopal Church, two with the Baptist, and two with the Presbyterian Church.

At the second De Camp reunion, June 1, 1870, in the after-dinner speeches, the Methodist clergy present, took great credit to their church for having developed so many stalwart Methodist characters, but it was reserved for the Presbyterian minister in the closing speech to give his Methodist brethren a parting shot, by reminding them that a godly Presbyterian mother laid the foundations of their excellent characters.

We can well imagine that Grandmother De Camp's recreations and pleasures were few, but we know that it was her privilege in 1842 to visit her New Jersey home under the filial escort of her son Harvey. It is related that her ten sons met her at the station to see her off, and each presented her with ten dollars for the journey. Willing granddaughters lightened her housekeeping burdens, among whom were Samantha Lindley, and Lucinda O'Neal.

Although raised a Presbyterian and connected with the neighborhood Church, she joined the Methodist Church at the time her husband did. Her last illness was of brief duration, lasting only seven weeks. "During all that period, and to the very last, she retained her mental powers unimpaired. Her intercourse with her children and grandchildren was of the most endearing character, and she conversed freely upon her approaching change, spoke of her confidence and the grounds of that confidence. She seemed to see her much-loved daughter, who died in the faith twenty-six years before, and exclaimed, "Phebe! beautiful Phebe! O blessed Jesus!" She died December 1, 1859, forty-seven years after her settlement on the old farm, and in the eightieth year of her age. Dr. D. W. Clark (afterward bishop) preached her funeral sermon.

Her grave is in the beautiful cemetery at Oxford, Ohio, and on the tomb is engraved:

> 𝕬 fond mother,
> 𝕬 loving wife,
> 𝕬 faithful friend.
> "Bless the Lord, O my soul: let all within
> me bless his holy name."

Born on a battle-field of the Revolution, her life was singularly sweet and peaceful. Only eight months younger than her husband, in death they were divided by only ten months, after a wedded life of over sixty years.

CHILDREN OF EZEKIEL AND MARY DE CAMP.

NAME.	BORN.	DIED.	AGED.
1. Phebe, ...	October 16, 1799, . . .	August 28, 1835, ...	36
2. Hannah, . . .	November 17, 1800,	November 20, 1888, . .	88
3. David, ...	August 1, 1802, ...	October 2, 1882, ...	80
4. Walter, ...	September 25, 1803, . .	July 29, 1882, ...	79
5. Hiram, ...	February 1, 1805, . . .	April 1, 1880, ...	75
6. John, ...	November 15, 1806, . .	January 21, 1842, . . .	36
7. Harvey, ...	November 25, 1807, . .	November 17, 1878, . .	71
8. Joseph, ...	August 2, 1809, ...	June 10, 1879, . .	70
9. Margaret, . . .	December 23, 1810, . .	January 7, 1854, ...	43
10. Henry, ...	August 9, 1812, ...	February 3, 1853, . . .	41
11. Daniel, ...	December 28, 1813, . .	April 3, 1884, . . .	71
12. James, ...	May 7, 1815, . . .	November 19, 1858, .	43
13. Moses, ⎞ twins,	December 11, 1816, .	February 17, 1827, . . .	10
14. Sarah, ⎠	December 11, 1816, .	November 2, 1851, . . .	35
15. Mary, ...	June 18, 1818, ...		
16. Lambert, . . .	January 17, 1820, ...	December 16, 1891, . .	72
17. Job, ...	March 11, 1822, ...	February 10, 1877, . . .	55

PHEBE DeCAMP HAND.

Born in Westfield, N. J., October 16, 1799.

Died in Butler County, Ohio, August 28, 1835.

PHEBE DE CAMP HAND.

PHEBE, the eldest child of Ezekiel and Mary De Camp, was born October 16, 1799, in Westfield, N. J., and died August 28, 1835, on the farm in Butler County, Ohio, in her thirty-sixth year, a victim to the cholera scourge, her husband, Gideon Hand, dying two days before of the same disease. Aunt Mary says, "Phebe was a Presbyterian, she was of dark complexion and slight figure, but pretty."

Her eldest son, Sylvester Hand, who was seventeen when she died, writes us as follows: "My recollection of my mother is, that she was a Christian of the old stamp, who taught her children the Catechism at home, and which I have never forgotten. She read to her children the Ten Commandments, and impressed on them the obligations they were under to God "

She married Gideon Hand, November 27, 1817, and six children were born unto them: SYLVESTER, MARY, ELLIS, HARVEY, ELIZABETH, and JOHN.

It is worthy of note that at this date—June, 1896—all six children of this eldest child are living (the youngest sixty-one, the oldest seventy-eight), the only instance of no break among the children of the seventeen.

Gideon Hand was a brother of Darby Hand, sons of Ellis Hand, whose second wife was Hannah De Camp, sister of Grandfather Ezekiel. Darby married Phebe's sister Hannah, niece and namesake of her aunt.

Our great aunt Hannah had no children, the Hand children being by the first wife of Ellis.

PHEBE De CAMP HAND'S FAMILY.

CHILDREN.   GRANDCHILDREN.

ANNA BELLE HAND.
    Born December 7, 1845.
    Married Samuel Hannaford,
        Cincinnati, 1873.
    She died March 20, 1883.

1. SYLVESTER HAND.
    Born October 15, 1818.
    Married Margaret Innes, 1845;
      and had three children.
    Address, St. Louis, Mo.

ALBERT L. HAND.
    Born August 16, 1849.
    Married Sadie Morris.
    She died November 22, 1887.

CHARLES EDWIN HAND.
    Born July 9, 1852.
    Married Ettie Cottom, 1872.
    Married second time to
        Mary Shook, 1890.
    Address, Cincinnati, O.

EMMA F. BARTON.
    Born February 12, 1846.
    Married Leonard H. Arm-
       strong, 1867.
    Address, Butler, Ky.

2. MARY HAND.
    Born December 3, 1820.
    Married Julius Barton, 1845;
      and had five children.
    He died July 21, 1864.
    She married Samuel Randall,
      1871; but had no children.
    Mr. Randall died September
      27, 1891.
    Address, Houston, Tex.

WILLIAM L. BARTON.
    Born March 23, 1849.

PHEBE DE CAMP HAND'S FAMILY.

GREAT-GRANDCHILDREN.   **GREAT-GREAT-GRANDCHILDREN.**

ALICE BELLE HANNAFORD.
  Born May 26, 1875.
  Married George A. Moore,
    1893.
  She died February 16, 1896.

MARGARET HANNAFORD.
  Born March 19, 1877.
  Died November 20, 1877.

EDGAR NORTHCOTT HANNAFORD.
  Born April 25, 1879.

AGNES SMITH HANNAFORD.
  Born March 25, 1881.
  Died September 13, 1882.

ANNA BELLE HAND.
  Born June 18, 1874.

ALBERT MORRIS HAND.
  Born July 28, 1876.

GEORGE WATSON HAND.
  Born March 8, 1878.

CHARLES EDWARD HAND.
  Born June 3, 1886.
  Died July 7, 1891.

JOHN W. HAND.
  Born September 28, 1874.

MARGARET HAND.
  Born December 8, 1880.

STELLA HAND.
  Born February 3, 1892.

FRANK HAND.
  Born January 11, 1894.

EDWARD L. ARMSTRONG.   ETHEL V. ARMSTRONG.
  Born March 25, 1869.   Born October 8, 1894.
  Married Anna Tinsley, 1893.

ARTHUR ARMSTRONG.
  Born September 14, 1870.

ROYAL V. ARMSTRONG.
  Born November 5, 1875.

WILLIAM J. ARMSTRONG.
  Born March 27, 1880.

EARL ARMSTRONG.
  Born March 19, 1886.

PHEBE DE CAMP HAND'S FAMILY.

CHILDREN.	GRANDCHILDREN
	MARY E. BARTON. Born February 19, 1852. Died December 3, 1861.
2. MARY HAND.—Continued.	ANNABEL BARTON. Born September 28, 1858. Married Edgar B. Estes, 1894 Address, Houston, Tex.
	CHARLES V. BARTON. Born February 14, 1862. Married Lizzie A. Bryant, 1891. Address, Houston, Tex.
3. ELLIS HAND. Born March 14, 1823. Married Ellen S. Evans, 1847; and had two children. Address, St. Louis, Mo.	CLARENCE LEVIN HAND. Born June 9, 1848. Died June 19, 1868. EMMA FRANCES HAND. Born August 5, 1850. Married Geo. Gerling, 1881.
	WILLIAM ELLIS HAND (twin). Born November 23, 1847. Married Mary Donald, 1876. She died — MARY ELIZABETH HAND (twin). Born November 23, 1847. Died August 11, 1857.
4. HARVEY HAND. Born November 4, 1826. Married Narcissa Berry, 1847; and had ten children. She died November 17, 1864. Married second time Frances Elizabeth Cook, 1865; by whom he had twelve chil- dren. She died August 1, 1891. Address, Beagle, Kan.	SARAH ISABELLA HAND. Born December 13, 1849. Married James H. Cook, 1869. Address, Angelica, N. Y.
	ASA HAND. Born August 20, 1852. Married Mary E. Warren, 1878. Cole Camp, Mo.

PHEBE De CAMP HAND'S FAMILY.

GREAT-GRANDCHILDREN.   **GREAT-GREAT-GRANDCHILDREN.**

FAITH BARTON.
   Born March 25, 1892.

WILLIAM HAND.
   Born August 17, 1877.

JAMES E. HAND.
   Born August 29 1879.

MARY LENA COOK.
   Born November 7, 1870.
   Died April 30, 1872.

JAMES ASA COOK.
   Born December 26, 1873.
   Married Amy J. Jennings,
      1895.

CHARLES ATWATER COOK.
   Born December 11, 1875.

WILLIAM HENRY COOK.
   Born September 1, 1879.

MAUD J. HAND.
   Born December 21, 1879.
   Died December 9, 1882.

FLOYD HAND.
   Born July 14, 1881.

CLYDE M. HAND.
   Born February 13, 1884.

EARL ASA HAND.
   Born May 5, 1887.

PHEBE DECAMP HAND'S FAMILY.

CHILDREN.   GRANDCHILDREN.

ASA HAND.—Continued.

ELLEN HAND (twin).
    Born March 6, 1854.
    Married Joseph Crockett.
    She died in 1873.

EMILY HAND (twin).
    Born March 6, 1854.
    Died May 7, 1854.

HARVEY HAND, JR.
    Born February 28, 1858.
    Married Mary Holloway,
        1880.
    Address, Windsor, Mo.

4. HARVEY HAND.—Continued.   JOSEPH HAND.
    Born January 28, 1860.
    Married Mary Ellis Cordry,
        1888.
    Address, Ionia City, Mo.

JANE HAND.
    Born March 11, 1862.
    Married James C. Carpenter,
        1880.
    Address, Ionia City, Mo.

ANNA FRANCES HAND.
    Born October 3, 1864.
    Died February 28, 1873.

CHARLES FRANKLIN HAND.
    Born August 9, 1866.
    Died March, 1873.

FREDERIC HARVEY HAND.
    Born September 12, 1868.
    Married Louisa Livingston,
        1891.

PHEBE DeCAMP HAND'S FAMILY.

GREAT-GRANDCHILDREN.

NELLIE HAND.
Born May 30, 1889.

ROY HAND.
Born March 23, 1893.

LILLIE SNOW HAND.
Born July 10, 1895.

GREAT-GREAT-GRANDCHILDREN.

MARY FLORENCE HAND.
Born September 8, 1881.

JOHN HARVEY HAND.
Born February 23, 1884.

JAMES E. HAND.
Born May 1, 1886.

MATILDA LOVENIA HAND.
Born February 20, 1889.

AZORAH LOVENIA CARPENTER.
Born September 13, 1881.

CHARLES HARVEY CARPENTER.
Born May 10, 1883.

MABEL AUGUSTA CARPENTER.
Born March 2, 1885.

AARON DE CAMP CARPENTER.
Born February 15, 1887.

NELLIE HAND.
Born January, 1893.

PHEBE DE CAMP HAND'S FAMILY.

CHILDREN.   GRANDCHILDREN.

EDWARD A. HAND.
    Born September 1, 1870.
    Married Dove G. Henness,
    1889.

ANSON E. HAND (twin).
    Born May 16, 1873.
    Died January, 1890.

ARTHUR I. HAND (twin).
    Born May 16, 1873.
    Married Opha E. Henness,
    1894.

JOHN A. HAND.
    Born April 19, 1875.
    Died January, 1887.

4. HARVEY HAND.—Continued.

CLARENCE C. HAND.
    Born August 15, 1878.
    Died June, 1879.

ROBERT L. HAND.
    Born December 27, 1880.

HARRY E. HAND.
    Born April 12, 1882.
    Died October, 1882.

FRANCES E. HAND.
    Born January 3, 1885.

ALVA HAND (twin).
    Born October 15, 1886.
    Died October, 1886.

EVA HAND (twin).
    Born October 15, 1886.
    Died October, 1886.

ANNIE E. STEVENSON.
    Born May 12, 1852.
    Married David J. Thomas,
    1872.
    Address, Cincinnati, O.

5. ELIZABETH HAND.
    Born October 19, 1830.
    Married Henry D. Stevenson,
    1848; and had three chil-
    dren.
    Mr. Stevenson died May 22,
    1868.
    Address, Cincinnati, O.

MARY KATE STEVENSON.
    Born July 25, 1856.
    Married W. H. Smith, 1880.
    Address, Mt. Vernon, N. Y.

CORA BELLE STEVENSON.
    Born November 1, 1859.

PHEBE DeCAMP HAND'S FAMILY.

GREAT-GRANDCHILDREN.	GREAT-GREAT-GRANDCHILDREN.

MAUD E. HAND.
     Born January, 1890.

KATE L. HAND.
     Born March, 1892.

MARION H. HAND.
     Born November, 1893.

HARRY ISHAM THOMAS.
     Born May 31, 1875.

PHEBE DeCAMP HAND'S FAMILY.

CHILDREN.   **GRANDCHILDREN.**

GIDEON D. HAND.
    Born November 11, 1859.
    Married Theodora Lousgues,
      1883.
    He died June 1, 1894.
    Address, South Bend, Ind.

SARAH EMELINE HAND.
    Born July 6, 1862.

6. JOHN D. HAND.
    Born May 16, 1835.
    Married Louisa M. Barrett, 1858;
      and had four children.
    Address, St. Louis, Mo.

    Married W. H. Ranstead,
      1881.
    Address, New Carlisle, Ind.

WILLIAM M. HAND.
    Born May 9, 1864.
    Married Mary B. Saunders,
      1889.
    Address, St. Louis, Mo.

EDWARD L. HAND.
    Born January 1, 1868.
    Married Mary Pomranka,
      1884.
    Address, St. Louis, Mo.

PHEBE DECAMP HAND'S FAMILY.

GREAT-GRANDCHILDREN.   **GREAT-GREAT-GRANDCHILDREN.**

WILLIAM LOUIS HAND.
>   Born February 2, 1886.

MARIE ESTELLE HAND.
>   Born December 20, 1887.

RAYMOND LEO HAND.
>   Born February 1, 1890.

MERRITT MONROE RANSTEAD.
>   Born May 21, 1882.

MABEL HAND RANSTEAD.
>   Born July 25, 1884.

WILLMA MAY RANSTEAD.
>   Born April 25, 1886.

OWENS HAND.
>   Born October 26, 1886.

EDWARD HAND.
>   Born April 26, 1889.

3

HANNAH DE CAMP HAND.

HANNAH De CAMP HAND.

Born in Westfield N. J., November 17, 1800.

Died in Butler County, Ohio, November 20, 1888.

HANNAH DE CAMP HAND.

HANNAH, the second child of Ezekiel and Mary De Camp, was born in Essex County, N. J., November 17, 1800, and came with her parents, brothers, and sisters, to Reily Township, Butler County, Ohio, in the fall of 1812, when this country was but a wilderness. She was a member of the well-known De Camp family of Reily Township. She was married to Darby Hand on the 30th day of March, 1820, who also came from New Jersey two years later. She died of old age and general debility on the 20th of November, 1888, aged eighty-eight years and three days. She died upon the same farm which she and her husband first settled after marriage, and in the same house in which she had lived for nearly sixty years. She was the mother of twelve children, five of whom survive her. She had twenty-three grandchildren, thirty-one great-grandchildren, and three great-great-grandchildren. She was a consistent member of the Methodist Church for fifty years, a good wife, a kind and indulgent mother, a good and sympathetic neighbor, and in all the relations of life, a true woman.

-"*M.*," *in Western Christian Advocate.*

Her husband was a successful farmer, owning over 600 acres in Butler County, and 300 in Indiana. He died August 19, 1874, aged seventy-eight. Their golden wedding occurred March 30, 1870.

On January 28, 1879, a reunion was held at Aunt Hannah's home, in the vicinity of the old De Camp homestead. She was in her seventy-ninth year, and there were present, besides scores of relatives, her surviving brothers David, Walter, Hiram, Daniel, and Lambert, with their wives and the only other sister, Mrs. Mary Wilkinson, with her husband; also the widows of the deceased brothers, with one exception. These reunions were times

36

of real gladness and affection, as nothing ever occurred that was permitted to cause dissension or estrangement among them.

Aunt Hannah was of large and noble frame and presence, with a strong and melodious voice, one of nature's noble women.

Her children were RACHEL, SARAH, REBECCA, SAMANTHA, HARRIET, MARY JANE, ELIZABETH, HIRAM, GIDEON, PHEBE, ELIZA, and CENITH ELLEN.

HANNAH DeCAMP HAND'S FAMILY.

CHILDREN.   **GRANDCHILDREN.**

1. RACHEL (" LOCKEY ") HAND.
   Born November 30, 1820.
   Married Elisha Wilkinson, 1836;
   and had one child.
   She died May 6, 1838.

ALFRED WILKINSON.
Born April 20, 1837.
Married Mary Ann Gard.
He died about 1883.

HARRIET ALEXANDER.
Born June 4, 1841.
Married Thomas Roll, 1857.
McGonigle, O.

2. SARAH HAND.
   Born December 23, 1821.
   Married Henry Alexander, 1840;
   and had seven children.
   Mr. Alexander died June 7, 1875.
   Address, Oxford, O.

NANCY JANE ALEXANDER.
Born May 13, 1843.
Married John Stephenson,
1859.
Address, Wood's Station, O.

HANNAH DeCAMP HAND'S FAMILY.

GREAT-GRANDCHILDREN.   **GREAT-GREAT-GRANDCHILDREN.**

SILAS L. ROLL.
  Born January 14, 1860.
  Address, Los Angeles, Cal.

FANNIE H. ROLL.
  Born September 30, 1861.
  Married William Gros, 1883.
  Address, Delphi, Ind.

WILLIE GROS.
  Born March 4, 1885.
  Died April 23, 1893.

PAULINE GROS.
  Born April 29, 1889.
  Died May 24, 1889.

JOHN L. ROLL.
  Born February 9, 1864.
  Died May 7, 1864.

HENRY A. ROLL.
  Born December 21, 1866.

NELLIE W. ROLL.
  Born October 26, 1874.

WILLIAM STANLEY ROLL.
  Born March 22, 1883.

WILLIAM H. STEPHENSON.
  Born August 10, 1861.
  Married Minnie Moore, 1885.
  Address, Millington, N. J.

WALTER STEPHENSON.
  Born July 28, 1886.

GEORGE STEPHENSON.
  Born November 25, 1863.
  Married Laura Silverthorne,
    1886.
  Address, Asheville, N. C.

SAMUEL STEPHENSON.
  Born August 9, 1868.
  Attorney, Great Falls, Mont.

DARBY STEPHENSON.
  Born April 16, 1871.
  Married Emma Garner, 1896.

JOHN STEPHENSON.
  Born March 21, 1878.

WAYNE STEPHENSON.
  Born September 22, 1881.

NELLIE STEPHENSON.
  Born September 10, 1884.

HANNAH DeCAMP HAND'S FAMILY.

CHILDREN.   GRANDCHILDREN.

{ LEWIS D. ALEXANDER.
　　Born February 9, 1845.
　　Married Elizabeth St. Clair,
　　　1865.
　　Address, Perkinsville, Ind.
　　He died April 13, 1882.

DARBY H. ALEXANDER.
　　Born October 7, 1847.
　　Married Martha Simmons,
　　　1872.
　　Address, Wood's Station, O.

2. SARAH HAND.—Continued.

MARTHA A. ALEXANDER.
　　Born June 13, 1849.
　　Address, Oxford, O.

JOSEPH ALEXANDER.
　　Born April 7, 1853.
　　Married Anna Schmeticar,
　　　1876.
　　Address, Koro, Ind.

LILLIE E. ALEXANDER.
　　Born April 1, 1856.
　　Married Isaac R. Kennard,
　　　1874.
　　Address, Delphi, Ind.

3. REBECCA HAND.
　　Born September 19, 1823.
　　Married M. T. Mustin, 1841;
　　　and had two children.
　　Address, Wood's Station, O.

JOHN LEONARD MUSTIN.
　　Born March 26, 1843.
　　Married Agnes Dalzell, 1869.
　　Address, Wood's Station, O.

MARY ADELAIDE MUSTIN.
　　Born August 15, 1846.
　　Died October 1, 1875.

HANNAH DeCAMP HAND'S FAMILY.

GREAT-GRANDCHILDREN. **GREAT-GREAT-GRANDCHILDREN.**

DR. WM. T. SHERMAN ALEXANDER.
  Born July 4, 1865.
  Address, Oxford, O.

HATTIE ALEXANDER.
  Born February 11, 1868.   MABEL JUNE DEAN.
  Married Thos. A. Dean, 1886.   Born June 27, 1887.
  Address, Perkinsville, Ind.

CORA BELLE ALEXANDER.
  Born April 3, 1869.
  Married Madison Prather,
    1892.
  Address, Anderson, Ind.

LEWIS ALEXANDER.
  Born August 3, 1870.
  Married Sareta Sharp, 1895.
  Address, Frankton, Ind.

LILLIE ALEXANDER.
  Born August 26, 1879.

CARRIE MAY ALEXANDER.
  Born February 5, 1877.

JESSIE ALEXANDER.
  Born August 2, 1882.

EDWARD ALEXANDER.
  Born January 6, 1877.
  Died August 25, 1881.

ALICE KENNARD.
  Born December 21, 1876.

Infant son.
  Born October 6, 1879.
  Died October 6, 1879.

CHARLES EDWIN MUSTIN.
  Born August 7, 1870.

CENITH ELLEN MUSTIN.
  Born August 23, 1873.

HANNAH DeCAMP HAND'S FAMILY.

CHILDREN.

GRANDCHILDREN.

ISAAC NEWTON LINDLEY.
Born June 4, 1845.
Married Carrie Williams,
1882.
Address, Hanford, Cal.

MARY LINDLEY.
Born December 4, 1846.

4. SAMANTHA HAND.
Born July 29, 1825.
Married John Lindley, 1844;
and had four children.
Address, Oxford, O.

LEROY LINDLEY.
Born October 19, 1848.
Married Ellen Roper, 1881.
Address, Hanford, Cal.

ELLIS HAND LINDLEY.
Born January 21, 1851.
Married Lida Jacobs, 1880.
Address, Wood's Station, O.

WILLIAM INNES.
Born February 21, 1848.
Married Cora J. West, 1878.
Address, Cincinnati, O.

EDWARD INNES.
Born May 13, 1850.
Address, Cincinnati, O.

5. HARRIET HAND.
Born April 13, 1827.
Married David K. Innes, 1847;
and had four children.
She died June 29, 1858.

FRANK INNES,
Born April 25, 1854.
Married Belle C. Oyler, 1885.
Address, Cincinnati, O.

HATTIE INNES.
Born February 12, 1857.
Married G. W. Coolidge,
1879; and have one child.
Address, Chicago, Ill.

6. MARY JANE HAND.
Born June 27, 1829.
Married George Kiles, 1855;
and had four children.
She died January 3, 1876.
He died November 2, 1893.

HANNAH J. KILES.
Born December 15, 1855.
Died June 17, 1857.

ADDIE KILES.
Born May 28, 1858.
Address, Oxford, O.

HANNAH DeCAMP HAND'S FAMILY.

GREAT-GRANDCHILDREN.   **GREAT-GREAT-GRANDCHILDREN.**

MARY ELLEN LINDLEY.
Born March 11, 1885.

EDITH LINDLEY.
Born June 22, 1883.

JESSE LEROY LINDLEY.
born July 29, 1884.

MAUDE LINDLEY.
Born January 25, 1887.

BESSIE LINDLEY.
Born June 22, 1889.

JOHN LINDLEY.
Born August 7, 1891.

RAYMOND GLENN LINDLEY.
Born September 23, 1887.

ELLIS IVON LINDLEY.
Born August 11, 1892.

EDNA INNES.
Born June 7, 1888.

RUTH INNES.
Born May 4, 1890.

INNES COOLIDGE.
Born May 9, 1880.

HANNAH DeCAMP HAND'S FAMILY.

CHILDREN.

6. MARY JANE HAND.—Continued.

7. ELIZABETH HAND.
   Born October 3, 1831.
   Died June 18, 1876.

8. HIRAM HAND.
   Born November 28, 1833.
   Married Nannie J. Birdwell,
   1857; and had six children.
   Address, Elwood, Ind.

9. GIDEON HAND.
   Born November 27, 1835.
   Died June 6, 1895.

10. PHEBE HAND.
    Born May 3, 1838.
    Married Benj. F. Stevens, 1856.
    Died April 3, 1857.

11. ELIZA R. HAND.
    Born August 18, 1841.
    Died August 2, 1874.

12. CENITH ELLEN HAND.
    Born August 17, 1844.
    Married David McGonigle, 1865.
    She died May 10, 1866.

GRANDCHILDREN.

JENNIE KILES.
Born January 26, 1861.
Died May 23, 1871.

ESTELLE KILES.
Born September 6, 1869.
Address, Oxford, O.

HANNAH H. HAND.
Born October 14, 1858.
Married Charles W. Dunlap,
1879.
Address, Siloam Springs,
Ark.

TIRZAH C. HAND.
Born January 20, 1861.
Died March 20, 1865.

DARBY T. HAND.
Born May 2, 1863.
Married Florence Beeson,
1883.

CHARLES W. HAND.
Born June 17, 1865.
Married Allie Elliotte, 1891.

FRANK B. HAND.
Born November 28, 1867.
Address, Pueblo, Col.

REBECCA ELLA HAND.
Born September 20, 1870.

CARRIE ELIZABETH HAND.
Born June 24, 1875.

HANNAH DeCAMP HAND'S FAMILY.

GREAT-GRANDCHILDREN.   **GREAT-GREAT-GRANDCHILDREN.**

WALTER H. DUNLAP.
   Born July 31, 1880.

MARY E. DUNLAP.
   Born March 14, 1888.

DAVID DE CAMP.

Born in Westfield, N. J., August 1, 1802.

Died at McGonigle, Ohio, October 2, 1882.

DAVID DeCAMP.

DAVID, the third child and first son of Ezekiel and Mary De Camp, was born in Essex County, N. J., August 1, 1802. He was one of seventeen children, and the eldest of twelve sons. He moved to Ohio with his parents in 1812, and in the midst of a wild and almost unbroken forest they pitched their camp on the spot in Butler County, Ohio, where now stands the De Camp homestead. Several years were here spent in assisting his parents in preparing the farm for cultivation. He afterward learned the trade of a bricklayer and plasterer, spending two years of his apprenticeship in work on the Miami University buildings in Oxford, Ohio; afterwards devoted himself to his trade for many years in Cincinnati. The religious advantages of his childhood were few, but the godly example of a devoted Christian mother, early led him to believe in the doctrines of Christ and to reverence his word. He was united in marriage to Miss Hannah Miller, October 12, 1824. In 1827 they were converted and admitted to the communion of the Presbyterian Church. After her death he married Miss Sarah Scudder, December 31, 1833. They moved to Cincinnati, and there united with the Methodist Episcopal Church in 1836. He was one of the number who organized Ebenezer, afterward Christie Chapel. He served the Church as chorister, trustee, steward, and class-leader, in which relations he was one of its most active workers and wisest counselors, allowing no interest of the Church to suffer from his neglect. His departure was a beautiful sequel to a life of consecration to the Master. God honored him with his constant presence, and gave him such visions of the saint's rest as filled him with joy and thanksgiving. After eight weeks' illness he slept in Christ, October 2, 1882, at McGonigle Station, Butler County, Ohio. He leaves a

48

wife, two sisters, two brothers, and many relatives to mourn
their loss, while the little Church of which he was a member
sorrow for " Uncle David" as for a father.

—*Rev. J. W. Mason, in Western Christian Advocate.*

After the death of Grandfather De Camp in 1860, David
De Camp removed to Butler County, and occupied the homestead and kept the farm for many years until it was sold, and
he removed to his house at McGonigle Station, Ohio. He had
the loving ministrations of a sweet-spirited and gentle companion, who had been a solace and blessing to him for nearly fifty
years. She died August 3, 1884. We have a most appreciative
memory of his love-feast experiences in Cincinnati in the
"fifties," being singularly gifted in the language of Canaan, and
melting all hearts with the music of his voice and the joy of
his soul.

His child by his first wife was ELIZABETH, and his children
by his second wife were CALEB and MARTHA.

4

DAVID DeCAMP'S FAMILY.

CHILDREN.　　　　　　　　**GRANDCHILDREN.**

1. ELIZABETH DeCAMP.
Born November 26, 1825.
Married James Coe, 1848; and
had three children.
He died February 22, 1869.
She died March 6, 1880.

WILLIAM ALVIN COE.
Born September 23, 1855.
Died October 20, 1856.

CLARA LILY COE.
Born January 26, 1861.
Married Faltine Steinmann,
1884.
Address, Reily, O.

ANNA BELLE COE.
Born June 14, 1865.
Died September 8, 1865.

BY SECOND WIFE.

2. CALEB DeCAMP.
Born October 4, 1834.
Died October 13, 1834.

3. MARTHA L. DeCAMP.
Born September 28, 1847.
Died October 12, 1851.

DAVID DE CAMP'S FAMILY.

GREAT-GRANDCHILDREN.   **GREAT-GREAT-GRANDCHILDREN.**

WALTER De CAMP.

———

Born in Westfield, N. J., September 25, 1803.

Died in Millville, Ohio, July 29, 1882.

WALTER DE CAMP.

WALTER, the fourth child of Ezekiel and Mary De Camp, was born September 25, 1803, in New Jersey. In 1821 he left home to learn the trade of a millwright. In 1825 he went to Huntsville, Alabama, where he became acquainted with Miss Sallie Bird, to whom he was married, March 4, 1827.

In 1831 he purchased and moved on a farm in Hanover Township, Butler County, Ohio, where he remained till 1880, when he moved to Millville, to live with his son-in-law Dr. Alfred Hancock and daughter Emeline. On July 29, 1882, he died of general debility. His wife died October 22, 1889, in her seventy-ninth year.

On March 25, 1827, he united with the Methodist Episcopal Church, of which he remained a consistent and active member until he moved to Millville, where he became a member of the Presbyterian Church. He was a man of extraordinary faith in the religion of the Holy Bible, of which he was a constant student. There was scarcely a text which he could not locate, and he could repeat chapter after chapter from memory; many of his favorite quotations were from the Psalms of David.

He was very conscientious in his dealings, ever governed by the principles of right and justice. He was emphatically optimistic in his views of matters and events. Whatever might transpire was for the best. However unfairly he might be treated by a neighbor, or however wicked an associate might be, yet he had charity for the same, and would reply with some Scripture quotation about " mild answers," " vile sinners," etc.

In politics he was far-seeing, nearly always ahead of public opinion; his opinions, being governed by justice and right, allowed him to occupy no middle ground, or to make terms with anything evil; hence he was found among the earliest of the anti-slavery people, and later in life he was a temperance worker and voted the Prohibition ticket. He was a liberal supporter of the Church, ever ready to lodge and feed the preacher; was first in any public enterprise, like the building of roads, churches, and school-houses. He placed a beautiful granite monument on his chosen burial-ground in Oxford Cemetery, leaving at death a very comfortable estate, the greater portion of which he had saved from the products of his farm.

—*Dr. W. D. Hancock, 1896.*

The teaching of a pious mother led Walter De Camp early in life to embrace Christianity. He professed the greatest faith in Jesus, his Savior, and the Holy Ghost, the Comforter. He was a leading member of the Methodist Church, in which he held every position, from simple membership up to that of licensed preacher. He has been a constant subscriber and reader of the *Western* from its earliest publication. During the last five years of his life he was a cripple from paralysis, and for convenience' sake, in attending divine service, became a member of the Presbyterian Church. Among his last words were, "I shall soon go to the mansion prepared for me in heaven."

—*Dr. Alfred Hancock, in Western Christian Advocate, 1882.*

Walter had but one child, EMELINE, a most attractive and hospitable lady.

WALTER De CAMP'S FAMILY.

CHILDREN.   **GRANDCHILDREN.**

DR. WALTER DE CAMP HANCOCK.
Born May 25, 1847.
Married Sallie Oliver, 1876.
Address, Millville, O.

1. MARY EMELINE DE CAMP.
   Born December 2, 1827.
   Married Dr. Alfred Hancock,
      1845; and had three chil-
      dren.
   She died September 24, 1893.
   He died August 19, 1888.

JOEL HANCOCK.
Born February 26, 1849.
Married Civilla Ent, 1873.
Address, Sheridan, Ind.

JAMES HANCOCK.
Born October 6, 1854.
Married Jennie Clippinger,
   1879.
Married second time to
   Lillie M. Laughlin, 1895.
Address, Celina, O.

WALTER De CAMP'S FAMILY.

GREAT-GRANDCHILDREN.   **GREAT-GREAT-GRANDCHILDREN.**

NELLIE B. HANCOCK.
> Born September 23, 1880.
> Died May 6, 1887.

BERTHA HANCOCK.
> Born May 7, 1876.

MARY BIRD HANCOCK.
> Born April 8, 1878.

ALFRED D. HANCOCK.
> Born June 17, 1880.

ELIZA HANCOCK.
> Born July 8, 1883.

CORA B. HANCOCK.
> Born February 10, 1886.

SALLIE O. HANCOCK.
> Born October 8, 1888.
> Died June 1, 1889.

GLEN H. HANCOCK.
> Born September 12, 1890.

JOSIE HANCOCK.
> Born September 24, 1881.

LEE BIRD HANCOCK.
> Born January 12, 1889.

HIRAM DE CAMP.

Born in Westfield, N. J., February 1, 1805.

Died in Cincinnati, April 1, 1880.

HIRAM DE CAMP.

HIRAM, the fifth child of Ezekiel and Mary De Camp, was born in Westfield, N. J., February 1, 1805, and died in Cincinnati, April 1, 1880. He was the first one of the sons to come to Cincinnati and work at his trade, that of a brickmason, at which he became very successful, being one of the foremost builders for many years.

The *Western Christian Advocate* of April 7, 1880, editorially noticed his death as follows:

"The Methodist Church in Cincinnati has lost another of its men of solid worth. Hiram De Camp died at his residence, April 1st, in the seventy-sixth year of his age. Mr. De Camp's final illness began with a congestive chill on Tuesday evening, March 23d, and until the day before his death he suffered intensely. His mind however was very clear, and only a few minutes before he died he plainly recognized one of his children who stood at his side.

"An hour before he died he asked for singing, and when his favorite song, 'Savior, more than life to me,' was started, he made a strong effort to join in the words, but, his power failing, he could only respond 'Amen, amen.'

"On Thursday morning, at 5.20 o'clock, surrounded by his beloved wife and his affectionate children—except one, whose severe illness kept her from his side—he breathed his last, leaving to all his affectionate farewell, and testifying in death, as he had done in life, to the saving power of Jesus' blood.

"Mr. De Camp was a lifelong Methodist, a member first at Wesley Chapel, Cincinnati, and then, for many years and until death, at Trinity."

Hiram De Camp was slender and tall, the tallest of the brothers. He possessed a most sympathetic and charitable nature, and was a most welcome visitor when trial or affliction came, never failing in comforting by his tender and loving words.

He was married January 14, 1834, to Elizabeth Hull, and his home life was ideal in comfort and affectionate regard, each for the other. His widow survives him in her eighty-second year, favored of the Lord, and surrounded by the loving care of a son and two daughters.

Their children were PHEBE, SARAH, CALEB, JOHN, HIRAM, JOHN WESLEY, ELLA, and GEORGE.

HIRAM DE CAMP'S FAMILY.

CHILDREN.

GRANDCHILDREN.

CARRIE E. MOORES.
Born June 18, 1856.

MARY C. MOORES.
Born January 21, 1858.
Died September 20, 1885.

1. PHEBE DE CAMP.
Born April 18, 1836.
Married James C. Moores, 1855;
and had four children.
She died June 28, 1865.

ALICE MOORES.
Born August 20, 1861.
Died December 22, 1864.

JESSIE PHEBE MOORES.
Born June 27, 1865.
Died August 18, 1865.

WILLIAM DE CAMP PERKINS.
Born June 2, 1860.
Died June 27, 1864.

GEORGE BASCOM PERKINS.
Born August 5, 1865.
Married Olive C. Reamy,
1895.
Address, Cincinnati, O.

2. SARAH DE CAMP.
Born August 16, 1838.
Married William T. Perkins,
1859; and had four children.
Address, Cincinnati, O.

HIRAM HOMANS PERKINS.
Born November 14, 1868.
Died May 25, 1870.

ELIZABETH PERKINS.
Born December 2, 1873.
Died June 2, 1874.

STANLEY CRANE DE CAMP.
Born June 30, 1877.

3. CALEB B. DE CAMP.
Born January 6, 1841.
Married Jennie E. Crane, 1865;
and had two children.
Address, Richmond, Va.

MARGERY DE CAMP.
Born April 2, 1883.
Died April 2, 1883.

4. JOHN WESLEY DE CAMP.
Born May 16, 1843.
Died March 16, 1848.

HIRAM DE CAMP'S FAMILY.

GREAT-GRANDCHILDREN.   **GREAT-GREAT-GRANDCHILDREN.**

HIRAM DE CAMP'S FAMILY.

CHILDREN.	GRANDCHILDREN.
5. HIRAM DE CAMP, JR. ·Born June 16, 1846. Married Viola Maley, 1874; and had one child. Address, Cincinnati, O.	GEORGE DE CAMP. Born January 10, 1876.
6. JOHN WESLEY DE CAMP (twin). Born March 21, 1850. Died June 4, 1850.	
7. ELLA DE CAMP (twin). Born March 21, 1850. Married J. E. Q. Maddox, 1874; and had two children. Address, Cincinnati, O.	MARY MADDOX. Born August 13, 1875. Died August 13, 1875. ROBERT D. MADDOX. Born July 14, 1876.
8. GEORGE DE CAMP. Born September 13, 1853. Died July 30, 1855.	

HIRAM DE CAMP'S FAMILY.

GREAT-GRANDCHILDREN.   **GREAT-GREAT-GRANDCHILDREN.**

JOHN DE CAMP.

Born at Westfield, N. J., November 15, 1806.

Died in Butler County, Ohio, January 21, 1842.

JOHN DE CAMP.

JOHN, the sixth child of Ezekiel and Mary De Camp, was born at Westfield, N. J., November 15, 1806, and died in Butler County, Ohio, January 21, 1842.

The following memoir by his pastor, Rev. David Kemper, is taken from the *Western Christian Advocate:*

"After an illness of twenty days, our beloved brother, John De Camp, the sixth child of Ezekiel and Mary De Camp, departed this life in full prospect of a blessed immortality, on Friday morning, January 21, 1842.

"With his parents he emigrated to Butler County, Ohio, in the fall of 1812, where he remained until his decease. On October 19, 1829, he chose a companion for life in Margaret Wilkinson, a sister of Mr. Gideon Wilkinson, with whom he lived most congenially.

"In 1837 the Lord severely afflicted one of his children. This affliction was sanctified to his good. On the recovery of the child, Brother De Camp began to read his Bible and pray in secret. He was invited to join the Church, but he replied, 'No, I will never join until I have obtained religion.' He went on in this way about a year, when he found that, instead of getting better, he got worse and worse. At length he resolved to have religion, if, in the mercy of God, it could be obtained.

"About this time a protracted meeting was appointed in the neighborhood of Zion meeting-house by Revs. Stroud and Wolfe. At this meeting he gave Brother Stroud his hand as a candidate for admission into the Methodist Episcopal Church, and also received a pardon for all his sins; and what added to his cup of rejoicing was, his wife joined the Church, and obtained religion at the same meeting. Soon after his conversion he was appointed class-leader, which office he filled with great acceptability and

68

usefulness for nearly four years. On the second day of this year he was attacked with the pleurisy, from which he suffered much; but he bore all with Christian fortitude. Often during his illness he was heard to say, 'All is well,' and frequently he praised God in ecstasies of joy.

"The writer of this visited him several times during the last week of his affliction. His conversation was almost entirely about religion and heaven. When it was thought he was dying, one of his brothers asked him if Jesus was precious? He triumphantly replied in the affirmative. He revived a little, and lived two days longer. When the time of his departure drew near, he called his wife, children, and friends around him, and, taking them by the hand, he bade them a long farewell, exhorting them to meet him in heaven; at the same time adding, 'Glory to Jesus! All is well!' At fifteen minutes past six o'clock A. M., he left this world of sorrow forever.

"From the time that Brother De Camp became a member of the Church, he appeared punctual and faithful in the discharge of all his duties, both at home and abroad. He was seldom, if ever, absent from the house of God on the days of divine service. In his death his companion has been bereaved of an affectionate husband, and his children of a tender father, and society of one of its most brilliant ornaments."

We were recently told of an incident in the life of John De Camp, worthy of record. While engaged in building old Zion Methodist Church, being a carpenter, he said, "We will put double joists under the 'Amen Corner,' because old —— gets so happy and shouts and stamps his feet, that I am sure he will go through the floor if we do not do it." After doing it, John De Camp was one of the first to be converted in the new church. His widow died March 23, 1886.

Their children were FRANCES, MOSES, RHODA ANN, ABIGAIL, ELMIRA, GIDEON, and WALTER.

JOHN DE CAMP'S FAMILY.

CHILDREN.　　　　　　　　　　　**GRANDCHILDREN.**

1. FRANCES DE CAMP.
   Born August 21, 1829.
   Married Jacob Stibbins, 1848;
   and had no children.
   She died October 18, 1886.
   He died September 4, 1865.

ALICE A. DE CAMP.
　　Born January 17, 1851.
　　Married William R. Morris,
　　　1872.
　　She died December 19, 1873.

JOHN DE CAMP.
　　Born November 21, 1852.
　　Died December 7, 1853.

HARRIET E. DE CAMP.
　　Born September 12, 1854.
　　Died September 6, 1872.

FRANCES M. DE CAMP.
　　Born September 3, 1857.
　　Died September 3, 1873.

2. MOSES DE CAMP.
   Born March 11, 1831.
   Married Mary J. Harper, 1850;
   and had seven children.
   She died June 11, 1872.
   He married second time to
   Kate Reed, 1876; but had
   no children.
   He died March 30, 1887.

MARY A. DE CAMP.
　　Born August 6, 1860.
　　Married George F. Martin,
　　　1880.
　　Address, Kokomo, Ind.

LAURA B. DE CAMP.
　　Born August 11, 1864.
　　Married William B. Hill,
　　　1888.
　　Address, Frankfort, Ind.

GIDEON W. DE CAMP.
　　Born May 10, 1867.
　　Died March 27, 1869.

JOHN DE CAMP'S FAMILY.

GREAT-GRANDCHILDREN.   **GREAT-GREAT-GRANDCHILDREN.**

EARL MARTIN.
  Born November 24, 1880.
  Died October 11, 1881.

EDWIN RAY MARTIN.
  Born May 5, 1882.
  Died September 21, 1884.

HOMER DE CAMP MARTIN.
  Born October 24, 1883.

STANLEY MARTIN.
  Born August 28, 1885.

PAULINE KATE MARTIN.
  Born July 21, 1888.
  Died September 22, 1895.

LOUISA IONE MARTIN.
  Born November 17, 1891.

REBA HILL.
  Born October 22, 1889.

MARY HILL.
  Born June 30, 1893.

JOHN De CAMP'S FAMILY.

CHILDREN.   GRANDCHILDREN.

GEORGE I. NEPTUNE.
 Born April 14, 1853.
 Married Ora Cones, 1878.
 Address, Memphis, Tenn.

MARTHA E. NEPTUNE.
 Born September 28, 1854.
 Married John Alford, 1875;
  who died October 18,
  1879.
 Afterwards married John M.
  Howard, 1883.
 Mr. Howard died April 15,
  1895.
 Address, Thorntown, Ind.

3. RHODA ANN DE CAMP.
 Born October 20, 1832.
 Married Richard Neptune,1852;
  and had three children.
 Address, Thorntown, Ind.

JOHN W. NEPTUNE.
 Born June 10, 1857.
 Married Nannie Moore.
 Address, Thorntown, Ind.

4. ABIGAIL DE CAMP.
 Born December 14, 1834.
 Married Samuel Ritter, 1857.
 She died August 18, 1859.

OLIVE HIDLEY.
 Born August 14, 1861.
 Married James M. Duncan,
  1881.
 Address, Reily, O.

5. ELMIRA DE CAMP.
 Born September 4, 1837.
 Married James P. Hidley, 1860;
  and had two children.
 Address, Reily, O.

MILTON L. HIDLEY.
 Born August 26, 1866.

JOHN De CAMP'S FAMILY.

GREAT-GRANDCHILDREN.   **GREAT-GREAT-GRANDCHILDREN.**

CARL I. NEPTUNE.
    Born June 3, 1879.

RICHARD C. NEPTUNE.
    Born September 21, 1880.

JOSEPH C. NEPTUNE.
    Born December 1, 1882.

TYLER G. NEPTUNE.
    Born May 11, 1886.

GEORGE DE CAMP NEPTUNE.
    Born January 19, 1890.

MARY NEPTUNE.
    Born December 27, 1892.

WILLIAM M. NEPTUNE.
    Born May 13, 1882.

WALTER G. NEPTUNE.
    Born April 20, 1884.

CELINE NEPTUNE.
    Born June 16, 1886.

HELEN NEPTUNE.
    Born May 13, 1889.

THEOPHILUS M. NEPTUNE.
    Born May 22, 1891.

CATHARINE NEPTUNE.
    Born April 11, 1894.

DOLORE B. DUNCAN.
    Born April 25, 1888.

MIRA A. DUNCAN.
    Born October 12, 1890.

JOHN DE CAMP'S FAMILY.

CHILDREN.	GRANDCHILDREN.

6. GIDEON W. DE CAMP.
   Born May 12, 1839.
   Married Sarah P. King, 1858;
   and had two children.
   He died November 27, 1879.

ANNA BELLE DE CAMP.
   Born August 18, 1860.
   Married Henry A. Wilkinson, 1877.
   Address, Oxford, O.

WALTER HARVEY DE CAMP.
   Born September 28, 1862.
   Address, Hamilton, O.

THOMPSON GRAY DE CAMP.
   Born March 2, 1863.
   Died August 14, 1888.

7. WALTER DE CAMP.
   Born May 12, 1841.
   Married Sarah E. Gray, 1862;
   and had three children.
   He died January 14, 1886.

MAGGIE DE CAMP.
   Born July 29, 1869.
   Married Frederick Fichter, 1889.
   Address, Hamilton, O.

JOHN GIDEON DE CAMP.
   Born October 19, 1877.
   Address, Hamilton, O.

JOHN DE CAMP'S FAMILY.

GREAT-GRANDCHILDREN.	GREAT-GREAT-GRANDCHILDREN.

DAVID HOMER WILKINSON.
    Born May 17, 1880.

ETHEL P. WILKINSON.
    Born October 17, 1882.

MARK WILKINSON.
    Born October 5, 1888.
    Died June 4, 1892.

MABEL D. FICHTER.
    Born November 6, 1891.

EDITH FICHTER.
    Born April 3, 1893.

HARVEY DE CAMP.

Born in Westfield, N. J., November 25, 1807.

Died in Cincinnati, November 17, 1878.

HARVEY, the seventh child of Ezekiel and Mary De Camp, was born in Westfield, N. J., November 25, 1807. He came to Cincinnati when seventeen, was apprenticed as a carpenter, and soon became one of the foremost builders of the city. He had many qualifications for leadership which found expression in the Church which he loved as the "apple of his eye." He was an ardent Methodist, holding all the official positions of a layman, giving freely of his time and money to further the interests of the Church, and was active in Sunday-school work. He was a friendly and wise counselor of the ministers, and his home was a Methodist headquarters for the itinerant. To him is ascribed the honor of inducing the Methodists to build St. Paul Church, which led Dr. Ridgaway, during the funeral services, to quote the epitaph of Sir Christopher Wren in St. Paul's Cathedral, London: "If you would see his monument, look about you." He died on November 17, 1878, and an editorial in the *Western Christian Advocate* of November 27th, contains the following:

"As an illustration of his character it may be stated that Harvey De Camp was never shaved on Sunday but once, and he never forgave himself for that. He never blacked his boots on the Sabbath, and on the Sunday he died he refused to cool his lips with ice until assured that it was purchased on Saturday. He never repeated a command to his children, and never promised them anything that he did not fulfill. When he announced to them his decision, he never changed it. He never rented a building without contracting that liquor must not be sold upon the premises, and would not permit any Sunday-selling or other immorality in a house owned by him. Withal, he was as simple as a child and as tender as a woman. His religious life was

78

full of sweetness. He was a most remarkable illustration of the value of strict parental training, and of the heroic practice of old-fashioned industry, morality, and religion.

"A series of highly appreciative resolutions were passed by the official board of St. Paul Church, and published in the daily papers of Cincinnati."

After amassing a competence as a builder and contractor, he became interested in paper-mills at Lockland, was a director in banks and various stock companies, and president of the Farmers' Insurance Co , a man of affairs to the last.

On May 2, 1829, he married Rebecca Ann Wright, who was the good and devoted mother of eight children, who hold her memory in loving regard. She died February 3, 1873. On the 9th of September, 1874, Mr. De Camp married Mrs. Sylvia A. Willis, who survives him, residing in Hartwell, Ohio, and is known as a capable leader in Methodist circles.

The children of Harvey and Rebecca De Camp were CHAR-LOTTE, MARY, MARTHA, ASBURY, LAURA, WILLIAM FLETCHER, ANNA, and JOHN.

HARVEY DE CAMP'S FAMILY.

CHILDREN.

GRANDCHILDREN.

HORACE H. JUSTICE.
Born June 12, 1849.
Married Clara S. Arnold,
1871 ; and had one child.
She died July 26, 1873.
He then married Millie P.
Mehling, 1875 ; and had
one child.
He married again Mattie
Rouzer ; and had three
children.
Address, Dayton, O.

1. CHARLOTTE DE CAMP.
Born February 25, 1830.
Married Enoch P. Justice, 1848;
and had two children.
He died September 15, 1851.
She married second time to
John Cohan, 1856; and had
four children.
He died June 10, 1876.
She died September 13, 1889.

ANNA REBECCA JUSTICE.
Born August 10, 1851.
Died July 19, 1852.

REGINALD HEBER COHAN.
Born April 18, 1857.
Married Maggie P. Dixon,
1878.
She died September 12, 1888.
He died October 9, 1890.

CHARLOTTE DE CAMP COHAN.
Born November 13, 1860.
Married Fred S. De Camp,
1885.
Address, Hartwell, O.

LAURA MAY COHAN.
Born July 26, 1868.
Died July 18, 1884.

WILBUR JUSTICE COHAN.
Born August 4, 1873.
Died August 26, 1875.

HARVEY DE CAMP STEVENS.
Born July 5, 1854.
Died September 7, 1874.

MARY EULALIA STEVENS.
Born April 18, 1856.
Married Wm. A. Lemmon,
1877.
She died February 23, 1895.

2. MARY ANN DE CAMP.
Born August 6, 1832.
Married Thos. Asbury Stevens,
1852; and had five children.
Address, Morrow, O.

MARTHA STEVENS.
Born June 26, 1860.
Died February 16, 1866.

JAMES BONTE STEVENS.
Born November 27, 1863.
Died April 7, 1866.

CHESTER NINDE STEVENS.
Born October 10, 1875.

HARVEY DE CAMP'S FAMILY.

GREAT-GRANDCHILDREN.   **GREAT-GREAT-GRANDCHILDREN.**

WILLIAM W. JUSTICE.
>Born March 13, 1872.
>Died March 20, 1873.

GEORGE LOUIS JUSTICE.
>Born December 17, 1877.

JOHN JUSTICE.
>Born February 10, 1886.

HORACE JUSTICE.
>Born March 29, 1888.

MATTIE C. JUSTICE.
>Born March 21, 1889.

MABEL P. COHAN.
>Born November 7, 1878.
>Died March 23, 1881.

CHARLOTTE R. COHAN.
>Born November 24, 1884.
>Died August 9, 1886.

EMMA M. COHAN.
>Born December 4, 1886.
>Died January 17, 1888.

EARL W. DE CAMP.
>Born July 17, 1886.

MILDRED LEE DE CAMP.
>Born October 29, 1891.

6

HARVEY DE CAMP'S FAMILY.

CHILDREN.	GRANDCHILDREN.

3. MARTHA DE CAMP.
   Born June 30, 1836.
   Died August 8, 1856.

4. ASBURY DE CAMP.
   Born October 6, 1839.
   Married Ella Whitehill, 1871;
   and had one child.
   He died July 5, 1879.

HARVEY DE CAMP.
   Born September 11, 1872.
   Died August 26, 1877.

5. LAURA JANE DE CAMP.
   Born June 23, 1841.
   Married Henry E. Holtzinger,
   1866; and had three children.
   Address, Cincinnati, O.

HARRY DE CAMP HOLTZINGER.
   Born October 13, 1868.
   Died May 15, 1896.

BERTHA BLANCHE HOLTZINGER.
   Born May 12, 1870.

MAYNARD F. HOLTZINGER.
   Born June 25, 1879.

6. WILLIAM FLETCHER DE CAMP.
   Born July 2, 1843.
   Married Mary S. Spear, 1866.
   She died February 20, 1873.
   He married Sue M. Pullen, 1874;
   and had four children.
   She died November 11, 1882.
   He again married Jennie M.
   Green, 1885; and had one
   child.
   Wife died November 17, 1887.
   Address, Cincinnati, O.

WILLIAM F. DE CAMP, JR.
   Born August 8, 1875.
   Died March 29, 1876.

HARVEY DE CAMP.
   Born August 13, 1877.

EMMA GOULD DE CAMP.
   Born July 29, 1879.

MARY EVELYN DE CAMP.
   Born June 2, 1881.

JENNIE MAY DE CAMP.
   Born October 19, 1887.
   Died November 20, 1887.

7. ANNA ELECTA DE CAMP.
   Born April 29, 1846.
   Married Theo. F. Spear, 1869;
   and had four children.
   Address, Cincinnati, O.

WILLIAM MORGAN SPEAR.
   Born October 18, 1870.

HARRY MAGILL SPEAR.
   Born February 27, 1875.

CLIFFORD MORTIMER SPEAR.
   Born April 7, 1880.

LAURA MAY SPEAR.
   Born September 17, 1888.

SARAH ALICE DE CAMP.
   Born February 13, 1870.
   Married George Seeger,
   1893.
   Address, Cincinnati.

8. JOHN R. DE CAMP.
   Born December 20, 1848.
   Married Adele Sowles, 1868;
   and had three children.
   She died July 21, 1892.
   Address, Cincinnati, O.

EDNA FRANK DE CAMP.
   Born November 18, 1871.
   Married Albert H. West,
   1892.
   Address, Chicago.

DAVID RALPH DE CAMP.
   Born November 19, 1877.

HARVEY DE CAMP'S FAMILY.

GREAT-GRANDCHILDREN.   **GREAT-GREAT-GRANDCHILDREN.**

ELIZABETH ADELE SEEGER.
  Born November 4, 1893.

EDNA DE CAMP SEEGER.
  Born February 7, 1895.

DOROTHY DE CAMP WEST.
  Born February 6, 1893.

KATHERINE CARTER WEST.
  Born December 4, 1895.

JOSEPH De CAMP.

Born In Westfield, N. J., August 2, 1809.

Died in Cincinnati, June 10, 1879.

JOSEPH De CAMP.

Joseph, the eighth child of Ezekiel and Mary De Camp, was born in Westfield, N. J., August 2, 1809. His parents removed to Butler County, Ohio, in 1812, where they resided till their death. Joseph at the age of eighteen years came to the city of Cincinnati, and learned the trade of carpenter, being apprenticed to Mr. Bonsall. He was married to Miss Maria Cassat, January 30, 1831, and was the father of nine children, five of whom survived him at his death, June 10, 1879.

In his early life, soon after reaching Cincinnati, he united with the Baptist Church, and was always active and conscientious in the discharge of his religious duties. For many years he was a deacon in the Freeman Street Baptist Church, and afterwards in the Ninth Street Baptist Church. Of a very tender and affectionate nature, he was always the first to offer his sympathy and his assistance to those in distress, and no sooner did sickness or misfortune visit his friends, than the click of his cane could be heard upon the pavement as he approached the house of the afflicted. He was most generous, and gave away much of his means in unostentatious charity. One incident will, perhaps, best illustrate his full faith in the religion he professed. Soon after his marriage he heard a very pathetic appeal for aid, and he had but half a dollar in the world. He gave it all, and went home and told his wife what he had done. She cried and said, " What shall we do. We have barely enough in the house for breakfast." He said, " Mother, the Lord will provide." After breakfast next morning he took his Bible, as usual, for family worship, and then there was a knock at the door. A lady asked, " Does Mr. De Camp, the carpenter, live here?" He said, " Yes." She said, " I wish you would come to my house and mend my cellar-door." He went, and the lady gave him a number of repairs to make, and he was busy for several days. He said, "Never from that time did I know what it was to want." He thus tested God's promise, and ever after had that faith "that works by love and purifies the heart."

He was for many years associated in business as a builder and contractor with his young brother Daniel, under the firm name of J. & D. De Camp, and that firm erected many of the large buildings, warehouses, and railroad depots in this city.

No attempt has been made by the writer to eulogize him. Such things were distasteful to him, and when on his death-bed, he gave strict injunctions to his partner to refrain from anything like eulogy. "Tell the simple truth about me," he said: "a eulogy over a dead man is as useless as a monument will be in the day of resurrection." He died full of years and full of faith in his Savior, conscious to the last and in full assurance of a happy eternity beyond the grave. E. L. D.

His wife died August 5, 1891.

Their children were CAROLINA, CHRISTOPHER, JAMES F., EZEKIEL, JOSEPH, OLIVE, FRANCIS, ALICE, and JULIA MARIA.

JOSEPH DeCAMP'S FAMILY.

CHILDREN.

GRANDCHILDREN.

1. CAROLINA DeCAMP.
   Born March 23, 1832.
   Died August 2, 1832.

WILLIAM JOSEPH DeCAMP.
Born July 29, 1854.
Address, Ludlow, Ky.

FRANK WILBUR DeCAMP.
Born March 19, 1857.
Died October 31, 1860.

ELLA H. DeCAMP.
Born April 1, 1860.
Died June 16, 1861.

2. CHRISTOPHER C. DeCAMP.
   Born May 25, 1833.
   Married Eleanor C. Harwood,
   1853; and had five children.
   He died June 17, 1866.

ADELAIDE LINN DeCAMP.
Born April 16, 1862.
Married William K. Red-
mond, 1885.
Address, Ludlow, Ky.

BERTHA GRANT DeCAMP.
Born March 15, 1865.
Married Walter L. Wells,
1886.
Address, Ludlow, Ky.

CLARENCE EASTMAN DeCAMP.
Born October 18, 1859.
Married Mamie E. Wood-
worth, 1884.
Address, Los Angeles, Cal.

3. JAMES F. DeCAMP.
   Born January 2, 1836.
   Married Abbie E. Jackson, 1859;
   and had one child.
   He afterwards married Ida M.
   Bill, 1867; and had two
   children.
   He died August 11, 1888.

WELLS BILL DeCAMP.
Born October 31, 1869.
Married Emma Strieder,
1892.
Address, Cincinnati.

IDA MALVIRA DeCAMP.
Born September 9, 1873.
Married James H. Brown,
1894.
Address, Knoxville, Tenn.

BENJAMIN CRANE DeCAMP.
Born November 3, 1863.
Married Helene R. Turner,
1890.
Address, Cincinnati.

4. EZEKIEL L. DeCAMP.
   Born December 23, 1837.
   Married Maggie B. Crane, 1859;
   and had two children.
   Attorney at Cincinnati, Ohio.

JESSIE DeCAMP.
Born October 13, 1866.
Married Lowry W. Statler,
1892.
Address, Piqua, O.

JOSEPH De CAMP'S FAMILY.

GREAT-GRANDCHILDREN. **GREAT-GREAT-GRANDCHILDREN.**

WILLIAM ARTHUR REDMOND.
Born April 20, 1886.

GEORGE RALPH REDMOND.
Born July 29, 1891.

CHARLES STANLEY REDMOND.
Born July 21, 1895.

EUGENE CUSTER WELLS.
Born August 10, 1887.

JESSE BUELL WELLS.
Born October 24, 1888.
Died October 24, 1888.

ELMER W. DE CAMP.
Born December 6, 1886.

JAMES FRANK DE CAMP.
Born March 27, 1888.

HERBERT DE CAMP.
Born August 27, 1894.

BENJAMIN C. DE CAMP.
Born August 11, 1892.

DAVID C. STATLER.
Born December 17, 1893

DE CAMP STATLER.
Born April 12, 1895.

JOSEPH DE CAMP'S FAMILY.

CHILDREN.

GRANDCHILDREN.

5. JOSEPH DE CAMP, JR.
   Born February 9, 1840.
   Died December 1, 1841.

6. OLIVE E. DE CAMP.
   Born May 2, 1844.
   Married Charles S. Morten, 1864;
       and had one child.
   Address, Riverside, O.

JOSEPH DE CAMP MORTEN.
   Born June 9, 1867.
   Married Grace Murray, 1891.
   Address, Cincinnati.

7. FRANCIS DE CAMP.
   Born January 13, 1845.
   Died November 4, 1848.

IDA ALICE MOFFETT.
   Born June 27, 1868.
   Married William B. Bryer,
       1889.
   Address, Chicago.

8. ALICE E. DE CAMP.
   Born February 1, 1847.
   Married Henry Moffett, 1866;
       and had four children.
   He died January 12, 1882.
   Address, Chicago.

FRANK DE CAMP MOFFETT.
   Born January 29, 1872.
   Married Cora L. Taylor, 1895.
   Address, Cincinnati.

JUDSON ANDREWS MOFFETT.
   Born January 8, 1876.

HARRY CLEMENT MOFFETT.
   Born July 3, 1879.

9. JULIA MARIA DE CAMP.
   Born May 28, 1849.
   Died May 5, 1854.

JOSEPH DE CAMP'S FAMILY.

GREAT-GRANDCHILDREN.   **GREAT-GREAT-GRANDCHILDREN.**

SUSIE LORAINE BRYER.
    Born March 16, 1892.

HOWARD LEAVITT MOFFETT.
    Born April 8, 1896.

MARGARET DE CAMP MISENER-HANLON.

Born in Westfield, N. J., December 23, 1810.

Died in Butler County, Ohio, January 7, 1854.

MARGARET DE CAMP MISENER-HANLON.

MARGARET, the ninth child of Ezekiel and Mary De Camp, was born December 23, 1810, in Westfield, N. J., and died January 7, 1854, in Butler County, Ohio, at the age of forty-three. We are indebted to her daughter Mrs. Harriet Weatherby, for this brief, but beautiful description:

"My mother was a medium-sized woman, of slender figure, with dark hair and bright dark-gray eyes. In disposition she was very cheerful and amiable, making every one happy around her. She was a member of the Methodist Episcopal Church at 'Old Ebenezer,' near Grandfather De Camp's homestead. She was a devoted Christian, and died a triumphant death, calling her children to her, and giving to each her blessing."

She was married the first time to George Misener, early in 1825, by whom she had four children: JACKSON, HARRIET, JOHN, and MARY MISENER.

Her husband dying January 13, 1835, she married Oren Hanlon in 1836, and seven children were born to this union: HARVEY, LUCINDA, SARAH, DAVID, WILLIAM, ELIZA, and ANNIE HANLON.

Mr. Hanlon died March 24, 1852.

We regret it was impossible to obtain any picture of Aunt Margaret; but Aunt Mary says "she was nice-looking."

95

MARGARET DECAMP MISENER'S FAMILY.

CHILDREN.

GRANDCHILDREN.

MARGARET ALICE MISENER.
Born December 25, 1853.
Died November 9, 1857.

HATTIE C. MISENER.
Born October 26, 1855.
Died October 22, 1857.

EVA MISENER.
Born September 11, 1857.
Died October 7, 1857.

LUNETTIE MISENER.
Born August 24, 1859.
Married Edward L. McGee,
1881.
Address, Bloomington, Ind.

1. JACKSON MISENER.
Born January 1, 1826.
Married Mary M. Smith, 1853;
and had eight children.
She died January 7, 1872.
Married second time to Nannie
A. Davis, 1873; and had two
children.
She died June 20, 1883.
Address, Bloomington, Ind.

EMMA A. MISENER.
Born October 1, 1861.
Married William E. Adkins,
1882.
Address, Bloomington, Ind.

JENNIE H. MISENER.
Born August 9, 1865.

MARY R. MISENER.
Born May 30, 1868.
Married Fred. E. Finley,
1892.
Address, Bloomington, Ind.

JOHN M. MISENER.
Born October 10, 1871.

WILLIAM H. MISENER.
Born September 12, 1875.
Died October 6, 1876.

CLARA E. MISENER.
Born May 30, 1880.

ELLA WEATHERBY.
Born April 17, 1855.
Married Joshua O. Howe,
1875.
Address, Bloomington, Ind.

2. HARRIET C. MISENER.
Born September 10, 1830.
Married Colman Weatherby,
1853.
He died April 15, 1888.
Address Bloomington, Ind.

IDA WEATHERBY.
Born July 26, 1857.
Died March 21, 1859.

HARRY C. WEATHERBY.
Born February 26, 1860.
Married Emma Kohlbry,
1890.
Address, Memphis, Tenn.

MARGARET DeCAMP MISENER'S FAMILY.

GREAT-GRANDCHILDREN.   **GREAT-GREAT-GRANDCHILDREN.**

LEON WIER McGEE.
Born April 26, 1882.

BENJAMIN J. McGEE.
Born February 13, 1885.

EUGENE ADKINS.
Born October 1, 1882.

ROSS M. HOWE.
Born July 8, 1876.

OWEN C. HOWE.
Born December 22, 1877.

LOUIS P. HOWE.
Born April 18, 1881.

ANNA A. WEATHERBY.
Born December 23, 1891.

MARGARET DE CAMP MISENER'S FAMILY.

CHILDREN.   GRANDCHILDREN.

DR. WILLIAM W. MISENER.
    Born November 22. 1852.
    Married Ella A. Bates, 1882.
    Address, Tacoma, Wash.

CHARLES E. MISENER.
    Born August 26, 1855.
    Married Lottie B. Douglass,
        1877.
    Address, Buffalo, N. Y.

CHRISTIANNA MISENER.
    Born April 22, 1858.
    Died May 7, 1858.

3. JOHN B. MISENER.
    Born April 11, 1832.
    Married Frances McCawley,   { ALICE L. MISENER.
        1852; and had nine chil-   Born May 12, 1860.
        dren.   Married Prof. William S.
    Address, Steilacoom City,Wash.   Arnold, 1881.
                                        Address, Tacoma, Wash.

JOHN B. MISENER, JR.
    Born December 1, 1862.
    Died September 23, 1864.

FRANCES MAY MISENER.
    Born June 18, 1865.
    Married Albert Whyte, 1889.
    Address, Tacoma, Wash.

GEORGE A. MISENER.
    Born October 2, 1870.
    Married Elizabeth Bartlett,
        1890.
    Address, Tacoma, Wash.

JACKSON HARVEY W. MISENER.
    Born August 25, 1873.
    Address, Bisbee, Ariz.

EDNA MAUD MYRTLE MISENER.
    Born March 2, 1876.

MARGARET DeCAMP MISENER'S FAMILY.

GREAT-GRANDCHILDREN.   **GREAT-GREAT-GRANDCHILDREN.**

EDNA MAY MISENER.
> Born February 17, 1883.

WALLACE MUNSON MISENER.
> Born August 12, 1886.

LENORE MISENER.
> Born September 20, 1890.
> Died September 23, 1891.

DOROTHY MISENER.
> Born March 7, 1894.
> Died April 11, 1895.

DORRIS MISENER (twin).
> Born March 7, 1894.

CHARLES E. MISENER, JR.
> Born March 5, 1878.

FRANCES ALICE ARNOLD.
> Born July 10, 1883.

ELLA AGNES ARNOLD.
> Born April 3, 1885.

MYRTLE MARGUERITE ARNOLD.
> Born December 10, 1887.

WILLIAM WALLACE ARNOLD.
> Born February 2, 1890.

JOHN ALBERT ARNOLD.
> Born August 23, 1893.

GEORGE BARTLETT MISENER.
> Born March 24, 1892.

DOROTHY MISENER.
> Born May 12, 1895.

MARGARET DeCAMP MISENER'S FAMILY.

CHILDREN.   **GRANDCHILDREN.**

ROMEO LEWIS PROTZMAN.
Born October 27, 1853.
Married Sallie E. Schwan-
inger, 1875.
Address, Dayton, O.

4. MARY E. MISENER.
Born January 18, 1834.
Married Wm. H. Protzman,
1852 ; and had five children.
He died June 13, 1880.
Address, Dayton, O.

CHARLES HENRY PROTZMAN.
Born July 22, 1856.

ANNA BELLE PROTZMAN.
Born December 1, 1859.

LIZZIE PROTZMAN.
Born October 3, 1863.
Died November 1, 1881.

JOHN BOYD PROTZMAN.
Born March 27, 1869.
Died March 17, 1871.

MARGARET DE CAMP MISENER'S FAMILY.

GREAT-GRANDCHILDREN.   **GREAT-GREAT-GRANDCHILDREN.**

ELLA DE CAMP PROTZMAN.
Born August 6, 1876.

ANNA BLANCHE PROTZMAN.
Born October 15, 1877.
Married John Heier.

EDNA MAY PROTZMAN.
Born October 13, 1879.

EMMA GRACE PROTZMAN.
Born December 29, 1881.

HARRY CLANCEY PROTZMAN.
Born October 18, 1884.

DANIEL LEWIS PROTZMAN.
Born February 26, 1887.

JOHN JACOB PROTZMAN.
Born December 20, 1888.

MAMIE ELLEN PROTZMAN.
Born August 14, 1890.

WILLIAM HENRY PROTZMAN.
Born November 17, 1892.

MARGARET DE CAMP HANLON'S FAMILY.

CHILDREN.

GRANDCHILDREN.

LILLIE BELLE HANLON.
Born March 22, 1858.
Died March 27, 1863.

CARRIE MAY HANLON.
Born November 11, 1863.
Died January 12, 1864.

BY SECOND HUSBAND—OREN
HANLON.

5. HARVEY D. HANLON.
Born August 10, 1837.
Married Ella M. Ogden, 1857;
and had five children.
He died September 19, 1894.
Wife died November 6, 1892.

GEORGE MARTIN HANLON.
Born September 17, 1866.
Died October 17, 1867.

WALLACE HANLON.
Born April 1, 1870.
Married Ellen Meier, 1889.
Address, Dayton, O.

OREN HANLON.
Born August 20, 1877.
Address, Dayton, O.

WILLIAM H. O'NEAL.
Born August 5, 1857.
Married Harriet E. Bridg-
ford, 1885.
Address, Oxford, O.

6. LUCINDA HANLON.
Born May 4, 1839.
Married Andrew Jackson
O'Neal, 1856 ; and had two
children.
Address, Oxford, O.

HATTIE LAVENIA O'NEAL.
Born July 26, 1859.
Married Frank Landon,
1876.
Address, Hamilton, O.

WILLIAM McCAWLEY.
Died in infancy.

CHRISTIAN McCAWLEY.
Died in infancy.

SARAH ALICE McCAWLEY.
Born July 28, 1863.
Married Walter S. Morgan,
1884.
Address, Denver, Col.

7. SARAH HANLON.
Born November 1, 1842.
Married Alexander McCawley,
and had eight children.
She died April 9, 1877.
He died February 9, 1890.

SAMUEL T. McCAWLEY.
Born June 1, 1866.
Married Clara B. Williams,
1893.
Address, Alhambra, Cal.

LIZZIE McCAWLEY.
Died in infancy.

MARGARET DE CAMP HANLON'S FAMILY.

GREAT-GRANDCHILDREN.   **GREAT-GREAT-GRANDCHILDREN.**

RUBY M. HANLON.
>   Born October 9, 1891.

RUSSELL HANLON.
>   Born December 12, 1893.

MORRIS H. O'NEAL.
>   Born September 4, 1886.

HARVEY J. LANDON.
>   Born April 8, 1877.

ANNA B. LANDON.
>   Born April 20, 1879.

ARTHUR L. LANDON.
>   Born September 23, 1880.

HERSCHEL RAY LANDON.
>   Born April 6, 1890.

MAY MARIE MORGAN.
>   Born January 21, 1885.

SARAH DE CAMP MORGAN.
>   Born July 27, 1887.

MARGARET DeCAMP HANLON'S FAMILY.

CHILDREN.   GRANDCHILDREN.

FANNIE MAY McCAWLEY.
   Born December 6, 1869.
   Married Dr. E. S. Imel, 1886.
   Address, Algiers, Ind.

7. SARAH HANLON.—Continued.

ALEXANDER McCAWLEY.
   Born November 6, 1873.
   Died March 23, 1874.

HATTIE McCAWLEY.
   Born April 11, 1875.
   Died November 6, 1879.

8. DAVID D. HANLON.
   Born August 5, 1843.

9. WILLIAM ASBURY HANLON.
   Born May 8, 1845.
   Died June 20, 1849.

10. ELIZA JANE HANLON.   ELIZA JANE SHOWERS.
   Born June 19, 1849.   Born February 22, 1868.
   Married William Showers, 1866;   Married Joseph M. Smith,
     and had one child.   1886.
   She died February 23, 1868.   Address, Bloomington, Ind.

11. ANNIE HANLON.
   Born June 3, 1852.
   Died June 21, 1854.

MARGARET DE CAMP HANLON'S FAMILY.

GREAT-GRANDCHILDREN.   **GREAT-GREAT-GRANDCHILDREN.**

ALICE ELIZABETH IMEL.
  Born April 16, 1888.

EDWARD STANTON IMEL, JR.
  Born October 15, 1889.

{ ETHEL SMITH.
{   Born September 19, 1889.

HENRY De CAMP.

———

Born in Westfield, N. J., August 9, 1812.

Died in Cincinnati, February 3, 1853.

HENRY DeCAMP.

HENRY, the tenth child of Ezekiel and Mary DeCamp, was a babe of six weeks when the family began their eventful journey to Ohio. Rescued from the suffocating feather bed en route, he grew to man's estate, dying at the age of forty-one. He learned the trade of a stone-mason, coming to Cincinnati while yet a boy, and was a fellow-apprentice with the late Hiram Powers, the famous sculptor. He found ready employment for his skill and energy in the rapidly-developing city in the "thirties" and "forties." His stoneyard was at the northeast corner of Fifth and Mound Streets, afterwards removed to the northeast corner of Barr and Mound Streets.

He was a Baptist, being one of the prominent members and founders, doing the stone-work of the old Freeman Street Baptist Church, since merged into the Lincoln Park Baptist Church, where his daughters are efficient workers. He was an earnest Christian man, of very firm convictions, and always ready to express his opinion, when asked, upon the leading questions of the day.

On March 10, 1837, he was united in marriage to Mary Jane Sargent. Like his brother John, and subsequently his brother James, Henry died at comparatively an early age, having lung and liver troubles, but he patiently bore the suffering of his long illness. His wife and daughters Annie, aged nine, and Henrietta, aged seven, together with his brother Joseph and nephews Columbus and Ezekiel, comforted his last days with tender ministries; Emma, the youngest daughter, being born five days after his decease.

Henry De Camp left behind him a fragrant name and memory, and we regret it was impossible to obtain a satisfactory likeness of him. His wife died December 21, 1880.

Their children were CHARLES, DAVID, ANNIE, HENRIETTA, GEORGE, and EMMA.

HENRY DE CAMP'S FAMILY.

CHILDREN.   **GRANDCHILDREN**

1. CHARLES HENRY DE CAMP.
   Born December 9, 1838.
   Died February 26, 1841.

2. DAVID S. DE CAMP.
   Born August, 1841.
   Died ———, 1843.

3. ANNIE MARIA DE CAMP.
   Born November 16, 1843.
   Married Arthur G. Umberger,
      1877.
   He died August 29, 1879; and
      left no children.
   Address, Cincinnati, O.

MARY B. PEET.
   Born August 2, 1867.
   Married Robert B. Lawson,
      1893.

WILLIAM T. PEET.
   Born October 30, 1869.
   Died November 19, 1875.

4. HENRIETTA DE CAMP.
   Born April 1, 1846.
   Married William Peet, 1866;
      and had six children.
   Address, Cincinnati, O.

ELLA A. PEET.
   Born December 3, 1871.
   Married William F. Cam-
      eron, 1891.

WALTER D. PEET.
   Born September 30, 1874.

EDITH PEET.
   Born June 1, 1877.

ALBERT PEET.
   Born June 17, 1880.

5. GEORGE SARGENT DE CAMP.
   Born November, 1849.
   Died October, 1850.

6. EMMA DE CAMP.
   Born February 8, 1853.
   Married Frank Baker, 1869; and
      had one child.
   Address, Brooklyn, N. Y.

FRANK ELMER BAKER.
   Born August 30, 1872.

HENRY DeCAMP'S FAMILY.

GREAT-GRANDCHILDREN.   **GREAT-GREAT-GRANDCHILDREN.**

HAZEL CAMERON.
   Born June 6, 1892.

WILLIAM FRANK CAMERON.
   Born March 6, 1894.

RALPH CAMERON.
   Born January 29, 1896.

DANIEL DE CAMP.

Born in Butler County, Ohio, December 28, 1813.

Died in Hartwell, Ohio, April 3, 1884.

DANIEL DE CAMP.

DANIEL, the eleventh child of Ezekiel and Mary De Camp, was the first child to be born in the new log-house in Butler County. At fourteen, he drove alone the two-horse team to the mills upon the Miami, a journey requiring two days for its completion. In 1833 he came to Cincinnati, having learned the trade of a builder under his brother John, at the old homestead. In 1835 he and his brother Joseph formed a partnership as J. & D. De Camp, builders, on Eighth Street, between John and Central Avenue, which continued until 1864. During its existence they built many residences, stores, school-buildings, and churches, the most prominent buildings being the depots and workshops of the Cincinnati, Hamilton and Dayton Railroad; also of the Indianapolis and Cincinnati Railway, the first Pike's Opera-house, Glenn's, Carlisle's, Bishop's, and Cleaney's business blocks, also residences in Glendale of Stanley Matthews, Mrs. Daniel McLaren, Robert Clarke, and Mrs. Dr. Patterson. In 1867 he organized the Hamilton County Building Association — the parent of Building Associations — of which he was president until his death. It improved Wesley Avenue, and laid out and built the park-like suburb of Hartwell. Mr. De Camp was president of the Taylor & Faulkner Manufacturing Co., manufacturers of building material, and was also at the head of the firm of De Camp, Levoy & Co., wholesale manufacturers of saddlery.

Mr. De Camp joined the Presbyterian Church in 1842, under the pastorate of Rev. Dr. Lyman Beecher. He assisted in organizing and building the Seventh Street Congregational Church, of which he was deacon and trustee. Upon moving to the suburbs, he connected himself with the Presbyterian Church. He was a high-minded, conscientious Christian gentleman, a self-made, self-educated man, his life crowded with work, but overcoming every obstacle that interposed between his resistless will and honorable success. The precepts of religion, early in-culcated, were the rule, and formed the undercurrent of his busy, useful life.

On July 23, 1835, he married Miss Ellen Lee, a native of the North of England. She united with Dr. Beecher's Church at the same time that her husband did, and made the spiritual journey together. She survived him a few years, dying March 2, 1888.

In addition to the above, gleaned from the Western Biographical Cyclopædia, we knew Uncle Daniel to be the courteous gentleman, sweet and gentle in disposition, most tender and indulgent towards his wife and family, and a most useful citizen. His illness was of but few days' duration, dying on the third of April, 1884, at his Hartwell home.

Their children were THOMAS, EVALINA, EDWIN, EMMA, ROBERT, LYMAN, ELLEN, DANIEL, ELLA, and FREDERICK.

DANIEL DE CAMP'S FAMILY.

CHILDREN.   **GRANDCHILDREN.**

1. THOMAS L. DE CAMP.
    Born July 24, 1836.
    Married Maggie Leonard, 1866;   EMMA J. DE CAMP.
    and had one child.   Born November 17, 1867.
    Wife died April 13, 1873.   Married William T. French,
    He married second time, Hattie   1886.
    Harding, since deceased.
    He died August 11, 1885.

2. EVALINA DE CAMP.
    Born September 3, 1838.
    Died October 17, 1838.

                                       ELLEN LEE DE CAMP.
                                          Born October 25, 1867.
                                       EDWIN F. DE CAMP, JR.
                                          Born December 24, 1869.

                                       MYRON E. DE CAMP.
3. EDWIN F. DE CAMP.   Born August 1, 1873.
    Born September 16, 1839.
    Married Carrie Wallace, 1866;   ELIZABETH MAY DE CAMP.
    and had six children.   Born January 23, 1876.
    Address, Willits, Cal.   Died August 18, 1877.

                                       FLORA LOUISA DE CAMP.
                                          Born July 10, 1878.

                                       CARRIE BELLE DE CAMP.
                                          Born October 12, 1881.

                                       ROBERT TAYLOR.
4. EMMA DE CAMP.   Born July 31, 1863.
    Born October 8, 1841.   Died February 5, 1864.
    Married George H. Taylor,
    1862; and had two children.   GEORGE H. TAYLOR, JR.
    She died January 22, 1888.   Born July 31, 1873.
                                          Address, Hartwell, O.

5. ROBERT O. DE CAMP.
    Born December 4, 1843.
    Died October 14, 1857.

DANIEL DE CAMP'S FAMILY.

GREAT-GRANDCHILDREN.   **GREAT-GREAT-GRANDCHILDREN.**

THOMAS M. FRENCH.
     Born October 24, 1887.
     Died November 12, 1891.

JAMES H. FRENCH.
     Born November 1, 1888.
     Died June 25, 1889.

GILBERT S. FRENCH.
     Born February 3, 1890.

ETELKA L. FRENCH.
     Born September 12, 1891.

ADELINE C. FRENCH.
     Born November 12, 1893.
     Died October 28, 1894.

DANIEL DeCAMP'S FAMILY.

CHILDREN. **GRANDCHILDREN.**

NETTIE M. DE CAMP.
Born March 27, 1879.

ELSIE L. DE CAMP.
Born April 6, 1881.

FRANCES A. DE CAMP.
Born August 4, 1882.

KATE S. DE CAMP.
Born August 12, 1884.
Died June 3, 1887.

6. LYMAN BEECHER DE CAMP.
Born February 4, 1846.
Married Frances Pierce, 1877; DANIEL DE CAMP.
and have nine children.   Born July 15, 1886.
Address, Alhambra, Cal.

RAYMOND L. DE CAMP.
Born December 21, 1887.

EMMA BOVARD DE CAMP.
Born September 17, 1889.

JOHN SAMUEL DE CAMP.
Born May 11, 1891.

DOROTHY DE CAMP.
Born November 11, 1894.

7. ELLEN DE CAMP.
Born March 30, 1848.
Died June 29, 1853.

8. DANIEL BAKER DE CAMP.
Born August 3, 1850.
Married Mary Adams, 1878.
Address, Hartwell, O.

9. ELLA DE CAMP.
Born December 12, 1853.
Died July 27, 1855.

EARL W. DE CAMP.
Born July 17, 1886.

10. FREDERICK STORRS DE CAMP.
Born August 12, 1858.
Married Charlotte D. Cohan, MILDRED LEE DE CAMP.
1885; and have two children.   Born October 29, 1891.
Address, Hartwell, O.

DANIEL DE CAMP'S FAMILY.

GREAT-GRANDCHILDREN.   **GREAT-GREAT-GRANDCHILDREN.**

JAMES DE CAMP.

JOANNA EVANS DE CAMP,

Wife of James De Camp.

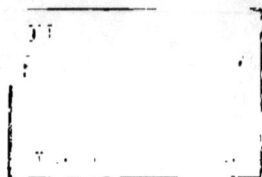

JAMES DeCAMP.

Born in Butler County, Ohio, May 7, 1815.

Died near Lockland, Ohio, November 19, 1858.

JAMES DeCAMP.

JAMES, the twelfth child of Ezekiel and Mary De Camp, was born at the Butler County homestead May 7, 1815. He came to Cincinnati in 1833, and learned the trade of a brick-mason, and soon became an efficient contractor and builder, noted for the thoroughness of his work and the fidelity of his engagements. In June, 1856, he purchased an interest in two paper-mills in Lockland, Ohio, removing to a farm near by; but the change in occupation was detrimental to his health, and he spent the year 1858 fighting consumption's grasp, trying the mild climate of New Orleans and the bracing air of Mackinac in turns, only to give up, with a feeling that if he could not be a well man, living at full tide of physical power, as he always had, he could not "play the invalid."

Fond of music, he was in his early married life a member of a band, but the associations were not helpful, and at this time—1842—the dying request of his brother John, "to prepare to meet his God," made a deep impression on him. This, with the prevailing prayer of his wife, caused him to quit the band. He gave his heart to God, was joyfully converted while walking on Seventh Street, near Plum. He joined the Fourth Street Methodist Episcopal Church, afterwards merged into Morris Chapel, and when—in 1849—Park Street Church (now St. John's) was colonized from Morris Chapel, he became its builder and one of its founders, where he was class-leader, steward, trustee, and treasurer until his removal to Lockland, where he identified himself with the Church in that village.

Although only in our thirteenth year when father died, we remember his faithfulness to the Church, going night after night, after a hard day's toil, leading the singing (carrying a tuning-fork), and speaking and praying with great fervor.

He was fond of hunting, and we recall him in his velveteen suit and cap, having molded the bullets and cut the wadding into suitable size, starting for a fortnight's sport after deer in Auglaize County. We often accompanied him to old Uncle David's on his squirrel-hunting visits.

It was a great trial for him to reconcile himself to dying and leaving his young wife, at thirty-seven, with nine children, the youngest a babe of seven months and the eldest a daughter of nineteen ; but Christ was precious to him and gave him the victory. He selected the hymns for his funeral, also the text of Scripture : "Not slothful in business, fervent in spirit, serving the Lord "—words that fitly described his character and life. At 6 o'clock on the morning of November 19, 1858, he was at rest.

His pastor, Rev. T. A. G. Phillips, in an appreciative memoir, wrote as follows :

"Many were the virtues of our departed brother. Affectionate and provident as a husband and father, he was, too, the fervent and devoted Christian man. An obliging and sympathizing neighbor, he was also the industrious and enterprising citizen, the prompt and punctual man of business ; so that he was prospered in the labor of his hand, as well as in his ' work of faith, and patience of hope, and labor of love.' In all the benevolent enterprises of the Church and of the age he not only felt a deep interest, but contributed largely of his means. His record is on high, while ' he rests from his labors and his works do follow him.' "

Father was happily married on May 20, 1838, to Miss Joanna Evans, and on her shoulders rested the care and responsibility of training her large family, and most worthily, with rare fortitude and foresight, did she perform her duty. She lived a widow thirty-seven years, dying most beautifully at her home in

Hartwell on the 23d day of April, 1895, at seventy-four, after a week's illness, during which time her children ministered to her in tender and constant service.

The children of James and Joanna De Camp were CELIA, CALEB, DAVID, JAMES, MORRIS, JOANNA, HENRY, LOUIS, and ROBERT.

JAMES DE CAMP'S FAMILY.

CHILDREN.

1. CELIA ELLEN DE CAMP.
   Born March 29, 1839.
   Married Alex. E. Line, 1866;
   and had five children.
   Address, Richmond, Ind.

2. CALEB OSCAR DE CAMP.
   Born February 24, 1841.
   Married Julia E. Voorhees, 1859,
   and had four children.
   Address, Cincinnati, O.

3. DAVID JOB DE CAMP.
   Born September 14, 1843.
   Married Celia E. Ashar, 1865;
   and had five children.
   He died March 7, 1895.

GRANDCHILDREN.

BERTHA KROELL LINE.
Born October 23, 1868.
Married George H. Binkley,
1893.
Address, Chicago.

FLORENCE ALEXANDRA LINE.
Born December 4, 1870.
Married Rev. William H.
Wise, 1895.

JOANNA EVANS LINE.
Born March 23, 1873.

JAMES DE CAMP LINE.
Born January 30, 1875.
Died May 4, 1876.

PAUL PERCY LINE.
Born May 15, 1877.
Died July 11, 1879.

IDA V. DE CAMP.
Born June 5, 1860.
Married Freedis P. Vorhis,
1881.

HARRY E. DE CAMP.
Born January 17, 1862.
Married Eleanor Mason,
1889.
Address, La Grange, Ill.

FRANCES H. DE CAMP.
Born February 19, 1866.
Married Harry Fox, 1886.
Address, La Grange, Ill.

JULIA I. DE CAMP.
Born March 2, 1871.

ETTIE DE CAMP.
Born June 24, 1866.

LAURA DE CAMP.
Born February 4, 1868.
Married George W. Van
Vranken, 1895.
Address, Schenectady, N. Y.

HERBERT C. DE CAMP.
Born April 5, 1870.
Married Maude C. Dyer,
1895.
Address, New Rochelle, N. Y.

EDITH DE CAMP.
Born June 24, 1877.

ROBERT JAMES DE CAMP.
Born June 21, 1879.

JAMES DE CAMP'S FAMILY.

GREAT-GRANDCHILDREN.   **GREAT-GREAT-GRANDCHILDREN.**

JOANNA ELIZABETH BINKLEY.
   Born June 18, 1894.

WILFRED VORHIS.
   Born July 7, 1883.

EDWIN MASON DE CAMP.
   Born July 17, 1890.

HARRY IRVING DE CAMP.
   Born April 1, 1894.

JAMES DE CAMP'S FAMILY.

CHILDREN.

4. JAMES MILTON DE CAMP.
Born December 25, 1845.
Married Jane A. Brandebury,
1867 ; and had two children.
Address, Cincinnati, O.

5. MORRIS BAKER DE CAMP.
Born February 15, 1848.
Married Jennie E. Johnston,
1868; and had three children.
He died July 24, 1875.
Address, Geneseo, N. Y.

6. JOANNA MILLER DE CAMP.
Born January 11, 1851.
Married Oliver E. Conner, 1869;
and had six children.
Address, Hartwell, O.

7. HENRY EVANS DE CAMP.
Born October 1, 1853.
Married Laura E. Welsh, 1889 ;
and had one child.
His wife died September 21,
1894.
Address, Cincinnati, O.

8. LOUIS COURTLAND DE CAMP.
Born April 9, 1856.
Married Sarah Cordelia Cowen,
1883 ; and had four children.
Address, Gardner, Col.

9. ROBERT SPENCER DE CAMP.
Born April 17, 1858.
Died August 26, 1859.

GRANDCHILDREN.

WALTER ALDEN DE CAMP.
Born April 27, 1868.
Married Caroline E. Middle-
ton, 1894.
Attorney at Cincinnati, O.

CHARLES BRANDEBURY DE CAMP.
Born July 20, 1874.

PEARLIE B. DE CAMP.
Born April 30, 1869.
Address, Geneseo, N. Y.

MORRIS MONTGOMERY DE CAMP.
Born April 2, 1871.
Address Buffalo, N. Y.

JAMES HART DE CAMP.
Born July 6, 1875.
Died November 7, 1875.

JOANNA DE CAMP CONNER.
Born October 12, 1869.

LOUIS E. CONNER.
Born October 28, 1873.
Attorney at Cincinnati, O.

ROBERT L. CONNER.
Born June 7, 1875.

OLIVER E. CONNER, JR.
Born August 12, 1877.

RUBY ELIZABETH CONNER.
Born October 5, 1882.

MARJORIE CONNER.
Born October 26, 1888.

ROBERT ERWIN DE CAMP.
Born October 17, 1890.
Died March 4, 1891.

ELSIE DE CAMP.
Born February 14, 1884.
Died November 12, 1885.

LOUIS EVANS DE CAMP.
Born October 24, 1887.

EDITH ALBERTA DE CAMP.
Born February 12, 1890.

JOSEPH ALFRED DE CAMP.
Born January 5, 1893.

JAMES DE CAMP'S FAMILY.

GREAT-GRANDCHILDREN.	GREAT-GREAT-GRANDCHILDREN.

MIDDLETON DE CAMP.
  Born October 22, 1895.

MOSES DE CAMP.

Born in Butler County, Ohio, December 11, 1816

Died in Butler County, Ohio, February 17, 1827.

Aged 10 years, 2 months, and 6 days.

SARAH DeCAMP ST. CLAIR.

Born in Butler County, Ohio, December 11, 1816.

Died in Butler County, Ohio, November 2, 1851.

SARAH DeCAMP ST. CLAIR.

SARAH, the fourteenth child of Ezekiel and Mary De Camp, and the twin-sister of Moses De Camp, Jr., was born in Butler County, Ohio, December 11, 1816, and died November 2, 1851, aged 35, yielding her life at the birth of her child, which also died.

In 1834 she married William St. Clair, and lived on the farm across the road from Grandfather De Camp's place. She and her husband were active and zealous members of "old Ebenezer" Methodist Episcopal Church. This was a famous and prosperous circuit charge for over fifty years.

Sarah was of somewhat lighter complexion than her sisters, and of a fleshy, heavy-set figure. Her daughter, Mrs. Dr. Charles N. Branch, writes us: " In the first place, my mother was blessed with a happy, cheerful disposition; was a devoted Christian. She was low of stature, with dark-brown eyes and auburn hair."

Mr. St. Clair died April 9, 1882.

Their children were MARY, PHEBE, MERINDA, SAMANTHA, JOHN, MARGARET, ELIZABETH, CHRISTIANNA, and three unnamed, dying at birth.

There is no picture extant of Aunt Sarah.

SARAH DE CAMP ST. CLAIR'S FAMILY.

CHILDREN.

1. MARY ST. CLAIR.
   Born August 12, 1835.
   Married Dr. Charles N. Branch,
   1857; and had three children.
   Address, Anderson, Ind.

2. PHEBE ST. CLAIR.
   Born February 11, 1837.
   Married William M. Davis, 1865;
   and had one child.
   Address, Milton, Ind.

3. MERINDA ST. CLAIR.
   Born November 19, 1838.
   Died October 22, 1839.

4. SAMANTHA ST. CLAIR.
   Born February 15, 1840.
   Married William Turner, 1862.
   She died in 1863.

5. DR. JOHN W. ST. CLAIR.
   Born December 12, 1841.
   Married Mollie C. Mosbaugh,
   1866; and had four children.
   Address, Milton, Ind.

6. MARGARET ST. CLAIR.
   Born October 24, 1843.
   Married Nathan Booth, 1869;
   and had three children.
   She died September 17, 1887.
   Address, Alexandria, Ind.

GRANDCHILDREN.

LILLIE B. BRANCH.
Born July 27, 1858.
Married Dr. Charles E.
Diven, 1874.
She died January 4, 1881.

JOHN H. BRANCH.
Born June 22, 1860.
Died August 11, 1868.

DR. CHARLES N. BRANCH, JR.
Born July 1, 1869.
Married Maud C. McCollough, 1892.

CHARLES DAVIS.
Born November 1, 1873.

GEORGE J. ST. CLAIR.
Born October 22, 1868.
Died September 27, 1875.

LAURA H. ST. CLAIR.
Born August 31, 1871.
Married Dr. Luke M. Gentle,
1894.
Address, E. Germantown,
Ind.

NORA O. ST. CLAIR.
Born September 16, 1873.

EVANGELINE M. ST. CLAIR.
Born March 4, 1876.

CLARA B. BOOTH.
Born December 28, 1869.
Died July 21, 1870.

WILLIE N. BOOTH.
Born December 24, 1873.
Died August 6, 1874.

CHARLES E. BOOTH.
Born December 10, 1875.

SARAH DE CAMP ST. CLAIR'S FAMILY.

GREAT-GRANDCHILDREN.   **GREAT-GREAT-GRANDCHILDREN.**

{ GEORGE R. DIVEN.
   Born April 1, 1876

{ MARGARET O. GENTLE.
   Born July 28, 1895.

SARAH DE CAMP ST. CLAIR'S FAMILY.

CHILDREN.   **GRANDCHILDREN**

DR. WM. T. SHERMAN ALEXANDER.
Born July 4, 1866.
Address, Oxford, O.

HARRIET ALEXANDER.
Born February 11, 1868.
Married Thomas A. Dean,
1886.

7. ELIZABETH ST. CLAIR.
Born May 1, 1845.
Married Lewis D. Alexander,
1865; and had five children.
He died April 13, 1882.
Address, Perkinsville, Ind.

Address, Perkinsville, Ind.

CORA BELLE ALEXANDER.
Born April 3, 1869.
Married Madison Prather,
1892.
Address, Anderson, Ind.

LEWIS ALEXANDER, JR.
Born August 3, 1870.
Married Sareta Sharp, 1895.
Address, Frankton, Ind.

LILLIE ALEXANDER.
Born August 26, 1879.

8. CHRISTIANNA ST. CLAIR.
Born July 20, 1847.
Married Joseph Yeager, 1866;
and had two children.
Address, Alexandria, Ind.

WILLIAM R. YEAGER.
Born August 22, 1867.

JOSEPH II. YEAGER.
Born June 15, 1872.
Married Stella L. Summers,
1895.

9. Infant, unnamed.
Died at birth, 1849.

10. Infant, unnamed.
Died at birth, 1850.

11. Infant, unnamed.
Died at birth, November 2, 1851.

SARAH DeCAMP ST. CLAIR'S FAMILY.

GREAT-GRANDCHILDREN.   **GREAT-GREAT-GRANDCHILDREN.**

MABEL JUNE DEAN.
   Born June 27, 1887.

MARY DE CAMP WILKINSON.

MARY DE CAMP WILKINSON.

Born in Butler County, Ohio, June 18, 1818.

MARY DE CAMP WILKINSON.

MARY, the fifteenth and sole surviving child of Ezekiel and Mary De Camp, was born in Butler County, Ohio, June 18, 1818.

In her sixteenth year she married Gideon Wilkinson, December 13, 1833, and moved at once into the substantial brick house on the farm, three miles from Oxford, which for sixty-three years has been her home.

Her husband was a successful farmer, having added to his possessions by dint of hard toil and good management, aided by the thrift of his wife, until his estate amounted to 780 acres—and beautiful land it is. He divided it shortly before his death among his children.

His death occurred March 13, 1891. It was his good pleasure, in June, 1887, in company with his son John, to prepare a reunion on his wife's sixty-ninth birthday, at which nearly two hundred of the relatives and neighbors were present to honor the occasion. Mary's sister Hannah, aged eighty-seven, was present; also her brother Lambert, aged sixty-seven.

We visited Aunt Mary in April, 1896, and found her looking hale and vigorous, and, barring some lameness from rheumatism in her feet, in the enjoyment of good health. She much resembles her father in looks—an honor that also belonged to her brother Harvey. She has always been a consistent member of the Methodist Episcopal Church, although now, for convenience, she attends the Presbyterian service at Reily.

Seven of her thirteen children are living, some of them close neighbors, and she is able to enjoy frequent visits among them.

She is a bountiful provider, and lives with her faithful and capable son John, whose birthday falls upon the same day as his mother's does.

As the golden sunlight of the twentieth century shall soon

lighten her pathway, may it be but a faint type of the golden glory of an eternity of blessedness awaiting her and hers!

On October 16, 1899, it will be just one hundred years since her sister Phebe first saw the light of day.

Her children were ABRAHAM, MIRANDA, ABIGAIL, RACHEL, ADELINE, MARY JANE, FRANCIS, REBECCA, JOHN, SARAH, HARRIET, GIDEON, and AMADORE.

MARY DE CAMP WILKINSON'S FAMILY.

CHILDREN.	GRANDCHILDREN.

MARY A. WILKINSON.
Born May 29, 1856.
Died January 6, 1870.

HENRY A. WILKINSON.
Born September 13, 1857.
Married Anna B. De Camp,
1877.
Address, Oxford, O.

1. ABRAHAM WILKINSON.
Born July 21, 1835.
Married Catherine Alexander,
1855, and had four children.
He died March 22, 1862.

LEWIS CALVIN WILKINSON.
Born February 24, 1859.
Married Anna M. Dillman.
He died July 31, 1892.

ABRAHAM D. WILKINSON.
Born June 24, 1861.
Died November 14, 1861.

WILLIAM EDWIN McCoy.
Born March 3, 1856.
Married Maggie B. Garner.
Address, Reily, O.

GIDEON W. McCoy.
Born March 25, 1857.
Married Metta M. Welliver.
Address, Reily, O.

2. MIRANDA WILKINSON.
Born November 3, 1836.
Married Samuel S. McCoy, 1855;
and had nine children.
Address, Reily, O.

ADA ELNORA McCoy.
Born January 12, 1860.
Married Butler L. Deneen.
Address, Reily, O.

ALBERT H. McCoy.
Born January 14, 1861.
Married Lizzie B. Beckett.
Address, Reily, O.

MARY DeCAMP WILKINSON'S FAMILY.

GREAT-GRANDCHILDREN. GREAT-GREAT-GRANDCHILDREN.

DAVID HOMER WILKINSON.
  Born May 17, 1880.

ETHEL P. WILKINSON.
  Born October 17, 1882.

MARK WILKINSON.
  Born October 5, 1888.
  Died June 4, 1892.

LOUIS HOWARD WILKINSON.
  Born December 30, 1884.

HENRY HERSCHEL WILKINSON.
  Born December 14, 1886.

FREDERICK McCOY.
  Born August 15, 1877.

MARY ELIZABETH McCOY.
  Born March 5, 1878.

ADDIE McCOY.
  Born September 12, 1881.

PEARL McCOY.
  Born April 21, 1883.

MYRTLE M. McCOY.
  Born April 17, 1888.

ROSCOE McCOY.
  Born September 19, 1886.

OMAHA DENEEN.
  Born September 6, 1877.

EMMA B. DENEEN.
  Born December 22, 1878.

LEROY DENEEN.
  Born June 13, 1880.
  Died July 15, 1881.

VANCE H. McCOY.
  Born December 20, 1887.
  Died May 26, 1892.

LEAH M. McCOY.
  Born May 16, 1889.

EVERETT N. McCOY.
  Born January 5, 1891.

ROBERT C. McCOY.
  Born April 23, 1894.

GERTRUDE M. McCOY.
  Born October 28, 1895.

MARY DeCAMP WILKINSON'S FAMILY.

CHILDREN.   **GRANDCHILDREN.**

JOHN W. McCoy.
Born March 13, 1862.
Married Dora Garner.
Address, Millville, O.

ANNA M. McCoy.
Born July 15, 1864.
Married James S. Morris.
Address, Reily, O.

2. MIRANDA WILKINSON—Continued.

LOUIS McCoy.
Born February 19, 1866.
Died May 20, 1866.

GERTRUDE McCoy.
Born August 7, 1873.
Married William Hopkins,
1891.
Address, Billingsville, Ind.

GEORGE McCoy.
Born February 2, 1876.

PROF. ORLANDO B. FINCH.
Born February 9, 1860.
Married Mary Dorrell, 1895.
Address, Oxford, O.

WILLIAM E. FINCH.
Born July 1, 1861.
Married Rosa A. Stevens,
1885.
Address, Oxford, O.

3. ABIGAIL WILKINSON.
Born March 9, 1838.
Married William J. Finch, 1859;
and had seven children.
Address, Oxford, O.

GIDEON W. FINCH.
Born June 7, 1863.
Married Caroline Hess, 1888.
Address, Oxford, O.

ELMER B. FINCH.
Born October 11, 1865.
Married Carrie Morrical,
1893.
Address, Oxford, O.

CHARLES L. FINCH.
Born January 11, 1868.
Married Mozella Knapp,
1893.
Address, Buffalo, N. Y.

MARY DeCAMP WILKINSON'S FAMILY.

GREAT-GRANDCHILDREN.　　　　　　**GREAT-GREAT-GRANDCHILDREN.**

EDITH P. MORRIS.
Born February 9, 1884.

HOMER HOPKINS.
Born July 4, 1892.

EMERSON EARL FINCH.
Born August 29, 1885.
WILLIAM E. FINCH, JR.
Born December 12, 1886.
GLADY P. FINCH.
Born August 5, 1889.
LEONA M. FINCH.
Born June 16, 1892.

AMOR V. FINCH.
Born July 31, 1893.

HELEN FINCH.
Born July 13, 1894.

BESSIE LEE FINCH.
Born April 26, 1894.
Died September 11, 1895.

MARY DE CAMP WILKINSON'S FAMILY.

CHILDREN.

GRANDCHILDREN.

3. ABIGAIL WILKINSON.—Continued.

> MARY E. FINCH.
> Born May 27, 1870.
> Married Edwin Morrical, 1890.
> Address Mixerville, Ind.

> ELLA FINCH.
> Born May 23, 1878.

4. RACHEL WILKINSON.
Born August 12, 1841.
Married Joseph B. White, 1861;
and had three children.
He died October 28, 1869.
She died April 2, 1876.

> CHARLES E. WHITE.
> Born January 21, 1862.
> Married Ida Monroe.
> Address, Onondaga, Mich.

> MARY ELIZA WHITE.
> Born August 22, 1864.
> Died December 26, 1866.

> JOSEPH B. WHITE.
> Born December 8, 1868.
> Address, Oxford, O.

5. ADELINE WILKINSON.
Born February 1, 1843.
Married John Weaver, 1866;
and had two children.
He died January, 1896.
Address, Reily, O.

> WILKINSON WEAVER.
> Born July 15, 1867.
> Married Jessie Bressler, 1892.

> HARVEY WEAVER.
> Born June 4, 1878.

6. MARY J. WILKINSON.
Born March 23, 1845.
Died May 7, 1845.

> ROENA H. WILKINSON.
> Born August 19, 1865.
> Died September 20, 1865.

7. FRANCIS M. WILKINSON.
Born November 30, 1846.
Married Nancy J. Reily, 1864;
and had eleven children.
Address, McGonigle, O.

> ANNA L. WILKINSON.
> Born March 27, 1867.
> Married John F. Hazeltine.
> Address, Hamilton, O.

> FRANKIE T. WILKINSON.
> Born June 12, 1869.
> Died July 30, 1869.

> ELLA R. WILKINSON.
> Born May 20, 1871.
> Died July 23, 1871.

MARY DeCAMP WILKINSON'S FAMILY.

GREAT-GRANDCHILDREN.   **GREAT-GREAT-GRANDCHILDREN.**

OTHO L. MORRICAL.
   Born August 4, 1891.

RUTH MORRICAL.
   Born August 12, 1893.

ELLA MORRICAL.
   Born June 7, 1895.

EVA WHITE.
   Born October 29, 1895.

CLYDE D. HAZELTINE.
   Born November 22, 1885.

NETTIE M. HAZELTINE.
   Born April 9, 1887.

MARIE HAZELTINE.
   Born October 14, 1888.

FRANK HAZELTINE.
   Born November 12, 1891.

MARGARET HAZELTINE.
   Born September 5, 1894.

MARY DE CAMP WILKINSON'S FAMILY.

CHILDREN.   GRANDCHILDREN.

REILY WILKINSON.
Born March 15, 1873.
Died August 10, 1873.

JAMES R. WILKINSON.
Born November 28, 1875.

HARRY H. WILKINSON.
Born May 6, 1877.

7. FRANCIS M. WILKINSON.—Cont'd.

ABIGAIL WILKINSON.
Born April 10, 1879.

WILLIAM H. WILKINSON.
Born November 27, 1880.

NANCY JANE WILKINSON.
Born May 13, 1883.

FRANCIS M. WILKINSON, JR.
Born March 13, 1885.

ARCHIBALD W. TRACY.
Born February 12, 1872.
Married Selma A. Moffatt,
1895.
Address, Hartford City, Ind.

8. REBECCA E. WILKINSON.
Born June 12, 1848.
Married David Tracy, 1871;
and had two children.
Address, New Castle, Ind.

MARY EUNICE TRACY.
Born December 3, 1877.

9. JOHN D. WILKINSON.
Born June 18, 1850.
Address, Oxford, O.

10. SARAH E. WILKINSON.
Born December 10, 1851.
Died March 8, 1853.

11. HARRIET E. WILKINSON.
Born June 26, 1856.
Married Oren Whipple, 1877;
and had two children.
She died November 12, 1887.
Address, Reily, O.

GUY WHIPPLE.
Born December 14, 1878.

IRA J. WHIPPLE.
Born October 19, 1881.

MARY DECAMP WILKINSON'S FAMILY.

GREAT-GRANDCHILDREN.   **GREAT-GREAT-GRANDCHILDREN.**

ARCHIE M. TRACY.
    Born November 20, 1895.

MARY DE CAMP WILKINSON'S FAMILY.

CHILDREN.

GRANDCHILDREN.

ALLAN G. WILKINSON.
    Born March 2, 1877.

RUTH T. WILKINSON.
    Born March 28, 1879.
    Married Isaac Woodruff,
    1896.

12. GIDEON J. WILKINSON.
    Born December 31, 1858.
    Married Eliza Gaston, 1876;
        and had four children.
    Address, Reily, O.

CRYSTAL BELLE WILKINSON.
    Born April 16, 1883.

HAMER D. WILKINSON.
    Born July 16, 1884.
    Died December 5, 1884.

13. AMADORE WILKINSON.
    Born January 22, 1861.
    Married Lewis Becket, 1881.
    She died August 2, 1884.

MARY DE CAMP WILKINSON'S FAMILY.

GREAT-GRANDCHILDREN.   **GREAT-GREAT-GRANDCHILDREN.**

LAMBERT De CAMP.

Born in Butler County, Ohio, January 17, 1820.

Died at Hartwell, Ohio, December 16, 1891.

LAMBERT DE CAMP.

LAMBERT, the sixteenth child of Ezekiel and Mary De Camp, was born in Butler County, Ohio, January 17, 1820. He came to Cincinnati in the spring of 1837, and served his apprenticeship as bricklayer with his brother Hiram. He was converted, and joined the Western Charge, Fourth Street Methodist Episcopal Church, in the fall of that year.

After a residence of seven years, on June 6, 1844, he married Elizabeth Folger, a woman of rare character and disposition. To this union five children were born, the last one. Elizabeth, April 26, 1854. A few weeks later, on June 1st, the mother died.

On September 4, 1856, he married Lydia Garwood, by whom he had five children. "He was a good man and true, possessing the respect and confidence of all who knew him."

He was for many years an active member of Trinity Methodist Episcopal Church, and was especially fond of music, being a fine singer. His last important business service was supervising the stone-work in the new Cincinnati Custom-house and Post-office.

He spent the last decade of his life in the beautiful suburb of Hartwell, near Cincinnati, where his widow survives him, full of gracious kindliness and activity in Church-work.

For years he and his brother Job—the two youngest of the seventeen—dwelt side by side in true brotherhood on Wesley Avenue, and formerly on Laurel Street, Cincinnati.

The death of his brother Daniel, in 1884, left Lambert, for seven years, the sole surviving brother.

FAMILY MEETING.

THE immediate relatives in Cincinnati and vicinity showed their affectionate esteem for him by visiting him in a body on the afternoon and evening of November 5, 1885, of which the papers spoke as follows:

"The residence of Mr. Lambert De Camp, in the beautiful

suburban village of Hartwell, was the scene last evening of a family reunion, which, for numbers in attendance and enjoyable gatherings, has never been excelled. In response to invitations issued among the members of this family, a very large number met at the Cincinnati, Hamilton and Dayton Depot yesterday evening. A special car was attached to the five o'clock northbound train for the accommodation of the party. One of the most pleasant features of the reunion was that the visitors were not expected, and the arrival of so numerous a congregation of relatives was an overwhelming surprise to Mr. Lambert De Camp. Greetings and congratulations usurped the first half hour after the visitors arrived. Then came one of the most interesting scenes of the evening. Mr. Ezekiel De Camp had been selected as the member of the family who should deliver an address expressing the greetings of those assembled, and also to bestow a token of love and esteem upon their beloved relative. This choice was happily made, and Mr. De Camp absorbed the attention of all for a short space of time. His manner and address were very pleasing.

" After his remarks there were renewed greetings, during which Mr. De Camp was presented with an elegant cane, and Mrs. De Camp with a handsome set of table china complete. The cane is an elegant ebony staff with a carved gold handle, on which is inscribed, ' Lambert De Camp, November 5, 1885, from his brothers' children.'

" The visitors had come well prepared to further the enjoyment with toothsome dainties. The adjoining residence, Mrs. Margaret De Camp's, was thrown open, and soon tables were groaning under the weight of luxurious dainties.

" Mr. Lambert De Camp is the survivor of twelve brothers, nine of whom have grown up and been closely identified with the history of Cincinnati. They were all mechanics, and, by a course of honorable and upright dealings, have secured to themselves a competency.

" Previous to the visitors dispersing to their several homes, a permanent organization, with a view of keeping a family record intact, and for the purpose of holding annual reunions, was effected. 'Mr. E. L. De Camp was selected as president, Mr. J. M. De Camp, secretary, and Mr. Hiram De Camp, treasurer.

"Among the members of the family present were: Mrs. Hiram De Camp, Mr. and Mrs. W. T. Perkins, Mr. and Mrs. C. B. De Camp, Mr. Hiram De Camp, Mr. and Mrs. J. E. Q. Maddox. Mrs. Sylvia De Camp, Mr. and Mrs. T. A. Stevens, Mr. and Mrs. Henry Holtzinger, Mr. and Mrs. T. F. Spear, Mr. and Mrs. W. F. De Camp, Mr. and Mrs. John R. De Camp, Mrs. Joanna De Camp, Mr. and Mrs. C. O. De Camp, Mr. and Mrs. James M. De Camp, Mr. and Mrs. O. E. Conner, Mr. Henry De Camp, Mrs. Joseph De Camp, Mr. and Mrs. James F. De Camp, Mr. and Mrs. Ezekiel L. De Camp, Mrs. Olive Morten, Mrs. Alice Moffett, Daniel De Camp, Mr. and Mrs. George H. Taylor, Mr. and Mrs. Lyman De Camp, Mr. and Mrs. Daniel De Camp, Lambert De Camp and wife Mrs. Lydia De Camp, Frank De Camp, Joe De Camp, Mrs. Margaret De Camp, Mr. and Mrs. Albert De Camp, and Mr. and Mrs. Horace Justice."

His funeral, in December, 1891, was from the Methodist Church in Hartwell, his pastor, Dr. Howard Henderson, officiating, assisted by his former pastor at Trinity, Dr. David H. Moore. His six sons were present, and bore him to his rest.

His children by his first wife were: CHARLES, WILLIAM, LYDIA, GEORGE, and ELIZABETH.

By his second wife: HIRAM, JOSEPH, ARTHUR, ANNA, and FRANK.

LAMBERT DE CAMP'S FAMILY.

CHILDREN.

GRANDCHILDREN.

MARY DE CAMP.
Born October 25, 1869.
Died June 28, 1870.

WILLIAM DE CAMP.
Born January 7, 1871.

LAMBERT DE CAMP.
Born August 3, 1872.
Married Alice Cunningham,
1894.

JESSE DE CAMP.
Born September 22, 1874.

SETH DE CAMP.
Born January 28, 1876.

1. CHARLES L. DE CAMP.
Born May 1, 1845.
Married Matilda L. Holmes,
1868; and had thirteen children.
He died April 11, 1896.
Address, Bellevue, Ky.

GEORGE DE CAMP.
Born November 22, 1877.

JOSEPH DE CAMP.
Born December 3, 1879.

ELIZABETH DE CAMP.
Born October 2, 1881.

HULDA DE CAMP.
Born April 24, 1883.
Died July 22, 1883.

MARTHA DE CAMP.
Born May 9, 1884.

CHARLES DE CAMP.
Born August 16, 1886.
Died April 11, 1896.

HORACE DE CAMP.
Born March 9, 1888.
Died March 9, 1888.

BENJAMIN DE CAMP.
Born September 25, 1889.

2. WILLIAM H. DE CAMP.
Born November 21, 1846.
Married Emma A. Felton, 1877;
and had two children.
Wife died December 29, 1880.
Married second time to Margaret K. Brown, 1883; and
had one child.
Address, Chicago.

MARY ADELAIDE DE CAMP.
Born January 27, 1879.

CYRUS FELTON DE CAMP.
Born December 16, 1880.
Died February 12, 1881.

GRACE FOLGER DE CAMP.
Born March 21, 1885.

3. LYDIA C. DE CAMP.
Born January 6, 1848.
Died January 6, 1848.

LAMBERT DE CAMP'S FAMILY.

GREAT-GRANDCHILDREN.   **GREAT-GREAT-GRANDCHILDREN.**

LAMBERT DE CAMP'S FAMILY.

CHILDREN.	GRANDCHILDREN.

4. GEORGE ASBURY DE CAMP.
    Born December 25, 1848.
    Died December 25, 1848.

5. ELIZABETH F. DE CAMP.
    Born April 26, 1854.
    Died June 26, 1854.

BY SECOND WIFE.

6. HIRAM A. DE CAMP.
    Born May 31, 1857.
    Married Claribel Brashears,
        1889.
    Address, Cincinnati, O.

DOROTHY DE CAMP.
    Born May 25, 1892.
    Died May 26, 1892.

LAWRENCE ELLINGTON DE CAMP.
    Born June 8, 1893.

VINCENT DE CAMP.
    Born March 3, 1895.

7. JOSEPH RODEFER DE CAMP.
    Born November 5, 1858.
    Married Edith Baker, 1891.
    Artist, Boston, Mass.

SARAH BAKER DE CAMP.
    Born July 24, 1892.

THEODORE LAMBERT DE CAMP.
    Born February 14, 1894.

LYDIA GARWOOD DE CAMP.
    Born September 27, 1895.

8. ARTHUR PAUL DE CAMP.
    Born July 28, 1860.
    Married Alice B. Tebbetts, 1886.
    Address, St. Louis, Mo.

9. ANNA MARY DE CAMP.
    Born October 31, 1863.
    Died February 13, 1866.

10. FRANK BAKER DE CAMP.
    Born July 8, 1866.
    Married Helen M. Jewett, 1891.
    Address, St. Louis, Mo.

ARTHUR LAMBERT DE CAMP.
    Born February 20, 1894.

LAMBERT DE CAMP'S FAMILY.

GREAT-GRANDCHILDREN.   **GREAT-GREAT-GRANDCHILDREN.**

JOB DE CAMP.

Born in Butler County, Ohio, March 11, 1822.
Died in Cincinnati, February 10, 1877.

Job, the seventeenth and youngest child of Ezekiel and Mary De Camp, was born near Oxford, Butler County, Ohio, March 11, 1822, and died in Cincinnati, February 10, 1877. In 1839 he came to Cincinnati, and entered into business relation with his brother James, and from that time until his death he resided in Cincinnati. He was married to Margaret B. Jacobs, May 8, 1844, who survives him. (Subsequently died, November 16, 1888, and was known for her goodness of heart and sweetness of disposition.) In 1842 he lost his brother John. This bereavement, in connection with the dying request of his brother that he would meet him in heaven, made an impression so deep that he determined to set about the work of seeking salvation, and he united with the Methodist Episcopal Church at the "Old Brick Church," then located on the corner of Fourth and Plum Streets. In the same year he was converted at the Duck Creek Campground. In 1848 he moved his membership to Christie Chapel. Soon after he was appointed a class-leader and steward. These two offices he filled with great acceptability and profit for nearly twenty-six years.

In the Sabbath-school he was an earnest worker for years. His straightforward frankness, joined with his ready sympathy with the young, made him a favorite with this class, and he was not only a useful Sabbath-school worker, but he was the chosen leader of the Young People's Prayer-meeting for years.

In his benevolent contributions he always devised liberal things.

The relations between him and his pastors were always of the warmest character.

He was the pastor's true friend. It was not the privilege of the writer to know the deceased in his strength and vigor. Our acquaintance began in, and was confined to, the narrow limits of

164

the sick-room. Brief, however, as it was, we may be indulged in noting some of the impressions there received. Perhaps the first and strongest was the simplicity of his Christian faith. We were impressed with his strong desire to live to do good, and yet such was his confidence in the wisdom of God that he was enabled to say, " The will of the Lord is done." We were further deeply impressed with his sturdy loyalty to his Church, and especially to his Church-home, Christie Chapel. We scarcely ever sat by his bed when he did not inquire, with tenderest concern, how the work was going. When he came to die, the light of life shone all around him, and his dying words were, "All is well! All is well!" .

—*Rev. William Runyan, in Western Christian Advocate.*

Job was not only indefatigable in his business and reaped the rewards of his diligence, but he had an unusually cheery and sunny disposition, bright, alert, and enthusiastic.

The children of Job and Margaret De Camp were EMMAZETTA, ALBERT, ELLIS, and ORIETTA.

JOB DeCAMP'S FAMILY.

CHILDREN.   **GRANDCHILDREN.**

1. EMMAZETTA JANE DE CAMP.
   Born December 16, 1846.
   Died September 7, 1849.

                                 ELLIS O. DE CAMP.
                                    Born April 4, 1874.
2. ALBERT JACOBS DE CAMP.
   Born July 16, 1850.
   Married Carrie Oblinger, 1873;   MARION DE CAMP.
      and had three children.   Born July 30, 1878.
   Address, Hartwell, O.
                                 ALBERTA DE CAMP.
                                    Born February 11, 1890.

3. ELLIS FAULKNER DE CAMP.
   Born August 31, 1852.
   Died August 31, 1871.

4. ORIETTA LEE DE CAMP.
   Born September 19, 1856.
   Died December 8, 1859.

JOB DE CAMP'S FAMILY.

GREAT-GRANDCHILDREN.   **GREAT-GREAT-GRANDCHILDREN.**

SUMMARY OF DESCENDANTS

OF

EZEKIEL AND MARY DeCAMP,

JUNE 1, 1896.

NOTE. —The relationship is to the grandparents and not to their children, as given throughout the book for family convenience.

CHILDREN.	GRAND-CHILDREN.		GREAT-GRAND-CHILDREN.		GREAT-GREAT-GRAND-CHILDREN.		GREAT-GREAT-GREAT-GRAND-CHILDREN.		TOTAL.
	Living.	Dead.	Living.	Dead.	Living.	Dead.	Living.	Dead.	
Phebe Hand, ...	6	0	24	15	46	6	1	0	99
Hannah Hand, ...	4	8	23	6	35	3	2	2	84
David De Camp, ...	0	3	1	2	0	0			7
Walter De Camp, ...	0	1	3	0	8	2			15
Hiram De Camp, ...	4	4	5	8	0	0			22
John De Camp, ...	2	5	11	6	23	4			52
Harvey De Camp, ...	5	3	15	12	4	10			50
Joseph De Camp, ...	3	6	13	2	1?	1			38
Margaret Misener-Hanlon, . . .	6	5	26	17	39	2			96
Henry De Camp, ...	3	3	6	1	3	0			17
Daniel De Camp, ...	4	6	17	3	2	3			36
James De Camp, ...	6	3	25	5	5	0			45
Moses De Camp, ...	0	0	0	0	0	0			1
Sarah St. Clair, ...	5	6	14	4	3	0			33
Mary Wilkinson, ...	7	6	34	10	34	4			96
Lambert De Camp, ...	5	5	17	6	0	0			34
Job De Camp, ...	1	3	3	0	0	0			8
17	61	67	237	97	214	35	3	2	733

Deduct descendants of second cousins recorded twice, ...   11

Total, ... 722

GRANDCHILDREN

OF

EZEKIEL AND MARY DE CAMP,

LIVING JUNE 1, 1896.

BORN IN 1818.

SYLVESTER HAND.

BORN IN THE 1820's.

MARY HAND RANDALL.
ELLIS HAND.
HARVEY HAND.
SARAH HAND ALEXANDER.

REBECCA HAND MUSTIN.
SAMANTHA HAND LINDLEY.
JACKSON MISENER.

BORN IN THE 1830's.

RHODA DE CAMP NEPTUNE.
ELMIRA DE CAMP HIDLEY.
ELIZABETH HAND STEVENSON.
JOHN D. HAND.
MIRANDA WILKINSON McCOY.
ABIGAIL WILKINSON FINCH.
HIRAM HAND.
HARRIET MISENER WEATHERBY.
JOHN B. MISENER.

MARY MISENER PROTZMAN.
LUCINDA HANLON O'NEAL.
MARY ST. CLAIR BRANCH.
PHEBE ST. CLAIR DAVIS.
SARAH DE CAMP PERKINS.
CELIA DE CAMP LINE.
EDWIN F. DE CAMP.
MARY DE CAMP STEVENS.
EZEKIEL L. DE CAMP.

BORN IN THE 1840's.

ADELINE WILKINSON WEAVER.
FRANCIS M. WILKINSON.
REBECCA WILKINSON TRACY.
DAVID D. HANLON.
JOHN W. ST. CLAIR.
ELIZABETH ST. CLAIR ALEXANDER.
CHRISTIANNA ST. CLAIR YEAGER.
CALEB B. DE CAMP.
HIRAM DE CAMP.
CALEB O. DE CAMP.
JAMES M. DE CAMP.

ANNIE DE CAMP UMBERGER.
HENRIETTA DE CAMP PEET.
LAURA DE CAMP HOLTZINGER.
WILLIAM F. DE CAMP.
ANNA DE CAMP SPEAR.
LYMAN B. DE CAMP.
JOHN R. DE CAMP.
WILLIAM H. DE CAMP.
OLIVE DE CAMP MORTEN.
ALICE DE CAMP MOFFETT.

BORN IN THE 1850's.

JOHN D. WILKINSON.
GIDEON J. WILKINSON.
ELLA DE CAMP MADDOX.
JOANNA DE CAMP CONNER.
HENRY E. DE CAMP.
LOUIS C. DE CAMP.

EMMA DE CAMP BAKER.
DANIEL B. DE CAMP.
FRED. S. DE CAMP.
HIRAM A. DE CAMP.
JOSEPH R. DE CAMP.
ALBERT J. DE CAMP.

BORN IN THE 1860's.

ARTHUR P. DE CAMP.

FRANK B. DE CAMP.

Total, 61.

VISIT TO PRESIDENT LINCOLN.

At the close of the Civil War, in March, 1865, a month before the death of President Lincoln, the eight De Camp brothers then living—David, Walter, Hiram Harvey, Joseph, Daniel, Lambert, and Job—went East in a body, enjoying themselves in New York City, stopping to visit relatives in the ancestral home at Westfield, New Jersey, where the Presbyterian Church was given them for Sunday evening service of praise and experience.

Upon visiting the Capital, they were introduced to President Lincoln by Judge William Johnston, of Cincinnati, as eight brothers, all of whom had voted for him and daily prayed for Divine guidance in his behalf. The President cordially shook hands with each one, saying a kindly word to each, and when he came to Job, the youngest, the President remarked that he envied him his name, as he needed patience. Job wittily replied: "But you have a better name already—Abraham, the father of the faithful."

It was at this period that the group-picture was taken, which is shown in this book.

170

FIRST DeCAMP FAMILY REUNION, JUNE 1, 1851.

[FROM THE WESTERN CHRISTIAN ADVOCATE OF JUNE 4, 1851.]

INTERESTING AND EXTRAORDINARY FAMILY SCENE.

BROTHER SIMPSON,—I have witnessed a family meeting, perhaps, in all its interests, unparalleled in history. The family was that of Ezekiel De Camp and his wife, Mary De Camp, who are now living in Reily Township, Butler County, Ohio. The family consists of the parents, seventeen children—twelve sons and five daughters. One son died at the age of ten years and two months. Sixteen lived to be heads of families. Two have deceased since their marriage. The eleven sons who grew to manhood all learned to be tradesmen, as follows: Four carpenters, five bricklayers and plasterers, one millwright, and one stone-cutter. All have become virtuous and prominent men in the Church of Jesus Christ and in their several trades and relations to society. There are nine of them living in Cincinnati; and, as to their mechanical labor, and almost every enterprise, whether social or benevolent, they are not surpassed by the same number of any other family. In the families of those sixteen children there are eighty-eight grandchildren now living, twenty grandchildren having died, making one hundred and eight grandchildren. Fifteen of these grandchildren have been married, one of whom has since died. In these fifteen families there are twenty-eight great-grandchildren living, two have died, making, in all, thirty great-grandchildren.

We have the following statistical account: Father Ezekiel De Camp, aged seventy-two years next October; Mother Mary De Camp, aged seventy-one years next June. Children living, fourteen; dead, three. Grandchildren living, eighty-eight; dead, twenty. Great-grandchildren living, twenty-eight; dead, two. Relations by marriage, living, thirty; dead, three. Making, living, one hundred and sixty-two; dead, twenty-eight. There were present, on this occasion: the parents, two; children, fourteen; grandchildren, eighty-two; great-grandchildren, twenty-two; related by marriage, thirty; in all, one hundred and fifty.

Six living grandchildren and six living great-grandchildren were
not present, making twelve. By adding those deceased, twenty-
seven, we have the remarkable family of one hundred and eighty-
nine persons, descendants from these two parents.

The parents invited this large family to pay them a visit,
which is the one I am trying to describe. A more interesting
sight I never saw. It was as interesting to some as the World's
Fair would have been, and perhaps more so. They all seated
themselves at the collation, which was very excellent and very
neatly arranged in the form of a hollow square, with a table in
the center. Around the center table the father and mother, their
brothers and sisters, with husbands and wives, who were present,
with the ministers and their families who were present, were
seated ; while the children, with their families and descendants,
were seated around the hollow square.

After they were all seated, the writer of this sketch then
made the above statistical account known to all present, and remarked briefly upon the following points :

1. The social relation or enjoyments of society : (1) Its happiness ; and (2) Its uses, from the care of parents to the interest
we feel in even acquaintances.

2. We must have a good, moral character, in order either to
enjoy happiness or impart it in the social relation.

3. That the gospel of Christ was the only system that taught
this relation and character, and was the only source of true joy—
the only way to heaven. There were of this family belonging
to the Christian Church, both parents, thirteen of the children,
and twelve of the grandchildren. We then invoked the blessing
of heaven upon the aged parents and all their descendants.

They then feasted heartily and pleasantly together, and divided the " Family Cake " among them. It was six feet in cir-
cumference, and worked in some beautiful devices on the top—
two hands in a grip of friendship, with the word " United " im-
mediately under—which were very expressive, and suited to the
occasion. At the close of the repast, a short address was given
by Brother Tenny—a Presbyterian minister of the New School—
very appropriate, and full of feeling. He dwelt upon the extraordinary meeting he was permitted to witness. Such a sight he
never expected again to witness. He had seen several meetings,

but none, in all its parts, agreed to this one. He then referred to the mercy of God in sparing the parents and children. He then spoke of a final meeting in heaven, where they would enjoy a happy meeting forever, and closed by a very appropriate prayer and benediction. All present, who had not partaken, were then invited to partake of the repast. After spending an hour or two in pleasant conversation, they parted, perhaps to meet no more till the great day.

REV. B. P. WHEAT.

REUNION OF THE DE CAMP FAMILY IN BUTLER COUNTY, JUNE 1, 1870.

[CINCINNATI COMMERCIAL, JUNE 2, 1870.]

A SPECIAL train over the Junction Railroad left the Cincinnati, Hamilton and Dayton Depot at half-past six o'clock yesterday morning, conveying the numerous members of the De Camp family to the old homestead in Reily Township, Butler County, for a grand family reunion, the first in nineteen years.

Arriving at Hamilton, a large deputation of relatives was taken from the down train from Dayton, and at half-past eight o'clock a mustering of the clans took place at Wood's Station, on the Junction Road, about four miles on the Hamilton side of Oxford. A number of carriages and wagons were in waiting at Wood's to convey visitors to the farm, where extensive preparations were already made to receive and entertain them. The homestead is a plain, substantial brick house, surrounded by a neat lawn, and well stocked for home support.

The novelty of the gathering together at one board two or three generations of one family, invested the occasion with unusual interest, nor was there one who saw it that will ever forget the sight. There were the very old, the old, the middle-aged, the young, all mingled in happy confusion, kindness and affection beaming from every countenance, and expressions of friendship flowing from every heart.

The lawn in front of the homestead was canopied with green branches shading the table, which was set for three hundred guests, and forming a hollow square, in the center of which stood a table, cruciform in shape, supporting a huge cake, a marvel of the confectioner's art, upon which were inscribed the baptismal names of the De Camp family, living and dead, commencing with the father and mother. The board literally groaned under the weight of viands, and was divided off into sections for each family, with the names conspicuously displayed on cards. After a few hours spent in social pleasure—pretty cousins coming in for an allowable amount of osculatory greeting—the older

174

and less sentimental comparing notes of experience overlapping forty years, the young fellows getting up an appetite on a game of base-ball that stood 21 to 23, and the babies enjoying the indisputable privilege of hearty squalling—dinner was announced, and the entire assembly seated themselves around the hospitable board. Harvey De Camp, of Cincinnati, gave the word of cheer, and bade his friends and kindred welcome. The venerable Father Wright, of the Methodist Episcopal Church of Glendale, invoked the Divine blessing, and then the feast began. Substantials and delicacies disappeared. Attentions were showered upon each other until an electric good feeling extended around the board, that flashed out from sparkling eyes, and hissed and hummed and buzzed in a thousand expressions of cordial fellowship.

Seated at the cruciform table in the center were relatives from New Jersey, several invited guests, and the following clergymen: Father Wright, William H. Babbitt, Glendale; W. X. Ninde, J. J. Thompson, F. S. DeHass, J. F. McClelland, Robert Vigeon, Cincinnati; William A. Robinson, Venice; and A. Bowers, Winton Place; and it will not be wondered if a newspaper reporter or two found their way to the guests' table.

Said Harvey, during the progress of the feast, "Our oldest brother, David, will cut the family cake;" and David, armed with a huge carver, expeditiously and skillfully demolished a hundred pounds of Keppler's sweetness, and sent it in bounteous subdivisions to the heads of families, to be tasted, and talked about, and subdivided again, like a wedding cake, for absent friends.

THE FAMILY HISTORY.

The De Camp family are of French-Huguenot origin. The Cincinnati branch came from near Westfield, New Jersey, in 1812, Ezekiel De Camp and his wife, Mary—the father and mother—having left that State for the "Far West" in that eventful year. They emigrated with ten children, and purchasing a quarter section of forest-land in Butler County, settled down to the hard and comfortless life of the pioneer. One acre only of the oak-forest was cleared, and upon this stood a log cabin. Indians lurked around, and made life hazardous; wolves howled at night, and made it hideous. The story of every pioneer's life was repeated in theirs. Their struggle amid the austerities and privations of uncultivated nature need not be related here. Suffice to say that, through it all, the father and mother instilled into the minds of their seventeen children—seven being born in Ohio— the principles of honesty and industry that have characterized them in public and private life ever since. The Bible was the family reading, and its precepts were inculcated with a clearness and fidelity that impressed them indelibly upon the young minds, and was never forgotten by them.

After the dinner yesterday, and the division of the family cake, Daniel De Camp formally called the meeting together, and, after briefly sketching the history of the family as given, read the following interesting statistics of the offspring of Ezekiel and Mary De Camp:

There are now living: children, ten; grandchildren, eighty- nine; great-grandchildren, one hundred and fifty-six; great- great-grandchildren, ten.

Dead: father and mother; children, 7; grandchildren, thirty- nine; great-grandchildren, forty-nine; added by marriage, ninety- three. Had all lived, the family would have numbered three hundred and sixty-three, and, including the additions by mar- riage, four hundred and fifty-six. Had father and mother lived to be as old as their parents, who also died on the Butler County homestead, they would have been permitted to see such a sight of progeny as few behold in this life—they having lived to the advanced age of ninety-three years.

There were present at the gathering one hundred and ninety- eight of the original stock; sixty-eight were absent. Of the connections by marriage there were sixty-three present, making a total of two hundred and sixty-one enjoying one of the most remarkable family reunions in the history of the West.

There has been no death in the family proper since 1858, and they are all remarkably healthy and vigorous.

The Cincinnati De Camps are Hiram, aged sixty-five years; Harvey, sixty-two; Joseph, sixty; Daniel, fifty-six; Lambert fifty; Job, forty-eight. They were all mechanics and builders, evidences of their skill and industry being seen in Trinity Meth- odist Episcopal and St. Paul Methodist Episcopal Churches; Wesleyan Female College; Carlisle's, Boylan's, Bishop's, Glenn's,

Cleneay's, and other large business blocks; in several common school-houses; and the depots of the Cincinnati, Hamilton and Dayton, the Indianapolis and Cincinnati, and Cincinnati and Marietta Railroads.

A social feature of the reunion yesterday was brief speeches by the clergymen already named, and, contrary to what may be popularly supposed, the clerical speeches sparkled with wit and overflowed with humor which no reportorial art may transfer to this cold and unsympathetic page. Interspersed with songs of praise heartily joined in by all, there was a jubilation felt which blood-warm sympathy only can afford. It seems profane to describe it, and, as a fitting finale, Ezekiel, one of the sons of Joseph, offered a resolution, which was adopted unanimously, that the De Camp Encampment be repeated at least every seven years in the time to come.

The happy meeting dissolved at six o'clock, and the special train returned to the city at eight o'clock last night, without a single circumstance occurring to mar its harmony or cast a shade of regret over the pleasant memory it will leave.